Wigs and Make-up for Theatre, Television and Film

Patsy Baker

Focal Press
An imprint of Butterworth-Heinemann Ltd
Linacre House, Jordan Hill, Oxford OX2 8DP

Ɋ A member of the Reed Elsevier plc group

OXFORD   LONDON   BOSTON
MUNICH   NEW DELHI   SINGAPORE   SYDNEY
TOKYO   TORONTO   WELLINGTON

First published 1993
Reprinted 1995

© Patsy Baker 1993

British Library Cataloguing in Publication Data
A catalogue record for this book is
available from the British Library

Library of Congress Cataloguing in Publication Data
A catalogue record for this book is
available from the Library of Congress

ISBN 0 7506 0431 X

Composition by Genesis Typesetting, Laser Quay, Rochester, Kent
Printed and bound in Great Britain by Scotprint, Musselburgh

Contents

Preface

I would like to express my gratitude to my daughter and her husband, Andrew and Nicola Bennett for their deciphering and typing of the manuscript, Mrs Christine Jones for her proofreading and professional help, Miss Jean Mitchell and Mrs Pat Fincham who sowed the first ideas for this book and gave me much encouragement and, above all, my husband Dennis Baker who has assisted and supported me during the time it has taken to write this book.

Patsy Baker

Introduction

This book has been written in response to the need for lecturers and students to learn the basic skills required to start work commercially within the varied branches of this industry. The requirements cover theatrical and media make-up together with postiche skills.

Hitherto the passing on of theatrical and media cosmetic skills has depended largely on short practical demonstrations by one make-up artist to another, mainly in the workplace. Postiche craft has always been taught as a separate subject and has usually not included the theatrical element. One area of knowledge without the other can spell boredom and loss of interest and has limited commercial value.

Now that the theatrical and media make-up has become an examinable subject there is a need for detailed explanations of the many and varied processes involved in the art and craft of these subjects. These comply with the requirements of both the International Health and Beauty Council and the City and Guilds of London Institute examinations and of the forthcoming National Vocational Qualifications.

I would not suggest that the methods referred to in this book are the only acceptable ones; neither would I wish to give the impression that every facet of the art of postiche making and theatrical and media make-up has been covered. The explanations have been simplified in order to allow the student to learn skills and colleges to run courses without the need for expensive materials.

This book is designed to lead you through the learning of these skills step by step by building up your knowledge and confidence in easy stages; assessment exercises are given at the end of each chapter. The text can be used by students learning on their own or in a group. You should always continue to practise and experiment on your own, applying what you have learned to develop your own ideas, techniques and skills.

Aims and scope of the book

This book aims to:

1 Provide a knowledge of a range of jobs and careers within the theatrical and media make-up and postiche industry.

2 Develop a basis for an informed assessment of personal aptitudes and attitudes in relation to theatrical and media make-up, and of postiche competences.
3 Develop a generalized command of the technology used in practical tasks so that students may progress to other applications of it in new tasks or new training without relearning.
4 Develop an ability to perform competently the practical tasks related to theatrical and media make-up as well as postiche work.
5 Develop the necessary competences in practical communication, task planning, carrying out tasks and checking the results of tasks.
6 Develop confidence in the new adult role.
7 Prepare individuals for professional qualifications by covering the syllabus for the International Health and Beauty Council's examination in theatrical and media studies together with City and Guilds wigmaking examination, and the National Vocational Qualifications.

This book covers training opportunities for:

- beauty therapists
- beauty specialists
- hairdressers
- drama students
- art students
- individuals – home based
- wigmakers
- theatrical and media make-up lecturers
- wigmaking lecturers
- actors and actresses – professional and amateur
- drama lecturers
- make-up artists

Equipment and make-up products

From a large roll of cotton wool prepare one bowl of 20 wet cotton wool pads/patters as follows:

Pads/patters

1 Unroll some cotton wool.
2 Cut off a large square.

3 Lay it flat in a large basin/bowl with a little water.
4 Lift the large square out carefully and squeeze out the excess water between the open palms of your hands, keeping the square open and flat.
5 Now take a pair of scissors and cut the square into small workable pieces.
6 Keep them damp by wrapping in cling film until required.

A box of cotton wool buds will be required for removing eye make-up.

General equipment

One tape measure.
One crêpe bandage.
One packet of orange sticks.
One small bowl of water.
One large bottle or jar of cleansing cream or lotion.
Eye make-up remover lotion.
One jar or tube of barrier cream for use on sensitive skins.
One bottle of astringent, e.g. witch hazel, skin freshener.
One box of tissues.
Skin coloured small plate or tile for mixing colours.
Small jar with cotton wool and disinfectant diluted with water.
Large cape/gown for client (black plastic).
Two hand-size towels.
Five small bowls for general use.
Two plastic spatulas, for removing cream from pots.
One wooden modelling tool, for modelling noses and scars.
Bottle of water-soluble matt spirit gum and ordinary spirit gum.
Eye dropper.
Scissors.
Tweezers and eyelash curlers.
Needles and cotton.
Children's white toilet soap (keep in a jar with a lid).
Jar of petroleum jelly.
Bottle of surgical spirit.
Bottle of acetone (nail varnish remover).

Hairdressing equipment

Hair band, hair net, cap, hair grips/clips etc.
Hair dryer, curling tongs, combs, brushes, rollers, lacquer and gel.

Foundation sponges

One packet of rounds or wedges of synthetic make-up sponges, used for applying foundation to the face and body.

Stippling sponges

Red rubber sponge, used for applying rubber-mask grease-paint on to latex.
Natural sponge, used for applying cake make-up.
Black stipple sponges or household sponges, used for applying special coarse skin effects with cream make-up, greasepaint, cake and soft tube make-up.

Brushes

Use artist quality sable brushes as follows:
Two narrow, sizes 2–4, for fine lines (round).
Two medium, sizes 7–9, for highlights/shadows (flat).
Two wide, sizes 10–12, for blending (flat).
One extra wide or round for powder.
One blusher.
One lipstick brush.

Note that cheap brushes have a short life because the hairs keep coming out. Sable brushes are expensive but will last a lifetime. One of each type of brush will be sufficient to start with.

One palette of 12 greasepaint colours

Kryolan Brandel 1004 range is very good. All the colours are intermixable. These are the answer to messy make-up boxes; they are easy to use and clean. Refills can be purchased for all colours. This palette is a *must* for the beginner.

One palette of 12 aquacolour wet make-up

Kryolan Brandel 1104 range. All the colours are intermixable using a little water. These are more difficult to master in technique. They are excellent for grease-sensitive skins, e.g. on children, although they can be too dry for some people's skin. Refills can be purchased for all colours.

One palette of 12 different lip colours

Kryolan Brandel 1204. Alternatively you could make do with a few collected lip colours.

Foundations

When beginning, choose one foundation colour to make you look very well tanned. This will work for most make-ups. The type of make-up that you choose is a matter of personal preference.

Supracolour   Cream base, manufactured from non-toxic oils and tested pigments. Strong colours are also available.

Paint-stick   Cream base. The ideal make-up for stage, film and television. Packed in propelling stick case which enables the make-up to be applied thinly and evenly.

Cake make-up   Compact cream-powder with strong colouring characteristics. Applied with a moist sponge. Will not rub off. The base contains ingredients of a moisturizing skin cream.

Aquacolour   Wet make-up. A water-based, grease-free compact make-up with good covering characteristics and containing valuable skin creams. Easily applied with a damp sponge and removed with soap and water. When dry, aquacolour should be carefully buffed by hand or with a soft cloth. It resists being rubbed off. Available in a wide range of shades.

Rubber-mask greasepaint   This is castor-oil-based greasepaint used primarily over latex caps, though it can be used over three-dimensional make-up as well. It is best to stipple on with a red rubber sponge. Never powder by rubbing or brushing but press a powder puff firmly down on the surface. Remove excess powder by brushing very lightly. If more colour is needed add it after powdering.

Clown white Leichner tin (a greasepaint)

Blood

You can buy blood but it is expensive. Instead you can make some up for yourself. The recipe is as follows:

● one cup of glycerine
● one teaspoon of red vegetable colouring

- half teaspoon of yellow vegetable colouring
- one teaspoon of non-toxic water-soluble red paint.

Mix well and pour into a container and seal until required. This may be swallowed if held in the mouth.

Tooth enamel

This is commercially produced and comes in shades of black, brown, nicotine, white, red and ivory. Never use on capped teeth or dentures.

Powder

Translucent powder.
White talcum powder.
Coloured blending powder: this is transparent, does not obscure the colour tones of the make-up, prevents smudging and sets the make-up.

Health, safety and hygiene practices

Make-up hygiene

Before starting work always cover work surface with clean paper. Place waste bin away from work surface. Use a trolley on wheels if available because it moves with you.

1 Wash brushes in neat mild soap, rinse well in water. Proprietary brush cleaner is also available.
2 Wash sponges in mild soap, rinse in clear water.
3 Clean moist make-up with a patter wiped across the surface.
4 Use a clean towel for each model/client.
5 Never allow your make-up box to get dirty.
6 Old sponges that have gone hard could harbour bacteria and irritate the skin. Sponges are cheap, so destroy them after your production.
7 Always use your own make-up and do not share it as this could transmit germs.
8 Always remove make-up gently. It is usually the removal of make-up that causes occasional skin irritation, not the make-up itself.

9 Always use cold cream on your face after taking off stage make-up, as this replaces the oils and moisture of the skin and helps prevent your face coming out in spots or rashes. This applies to male and female faces.

10 If a face still suffers from irritation and you have a fridge, try cold damp hand towels. This quickly cools the skin and stops the irritation (see Chapter 2).

11 If a person's skin is very sensitive to certain types of make-up, a barrier cream or lotion should be applied before starting the make-up.

12 Clean and tidy materials and surfaces as you work.

I should say at this point that unfortunately with some forms of theatrical and media make-up the actors do have to put up with a certain amount of discomfort for the sake of their art. It is only fair that as a make-up artist you should experience and be aware of this so as to render as little discomfort and as much sympathy as possible.

Model's requirements

1 Always be aware of your model's comfort and needs.

2 Ask if he/she is too warm or too cold.

3 Enquire if his/her seating position is comfortable. The model's back, neck and feet should be supported because some make-up can take hours to complete. You must remember that the model has a performance to give afterwards.

4 Speed and accuracy are very important. Forward planning is the key to saving time and tempers.

5 Make sure your model is well covered with a gown.

6 Protect your model's hairline with a hair band, and cover the hair completely using a large soft cap. Hair is usually dressed after the make-up and must always be protected against grease.

7 Protect the model by removing his/her earrings and rings, watches, eyeglasses and contact lenses. Place items in a box/bowl until make-up is completed.

8 Provide a safe place for the model's larger personal belongings.

9 Inform the model where the nearest lavatory and wash basin are situated.

10 A balanced temperament is required to keep nervous actors and actresses cool when under pressure.

11 Be prepared to offer refreshment during the course of a long make-up.

12 A work sheet should always be prepared and filled in before you start work and should be filed for future reference. A photograph of the work would help your memory considerably, especially if you have to repeat the make-up again at some later time.

13 A first-aid box should be available. It should contain the following:
- Burn dressings.
- Absorbent dressings in sealed sterile packs.
- Cotton wool.
- Absorbent lint.
- Bandages for head and fingers and a sling.
- Adhesive dressing strip.
- Scissors.
- Antiseptic lotion.
- 2% boric acid lotion.
- 2% sodium hydrogen carbonate lotion.
- Eyebath.
- Pair of dry rubber gloves.

14 You will need a good strong light to work under.

2 Cleansing and basic cosmetic make-up

Personal hygiene and presentation

Wear an overall or apron.
Tie long hair back from your face.
Remove jewellery – dress rings, neck chains and bracelets
(wedding rings are acceptable).
Cut long nails.
Check breath and perspiration.
Wash hands before and after work.
Wear sensible shoes, e.g. shoes that have a medium heel, and
are made of leather uppers which allow your feet to breath,
and also give good support. Avoid open strap shoes which do
not offer enough protection if you drop something on your
feet.

Introduction to cleansing

The face may be cleansed using one of the following products:

- milks and lotions: really best for oily skins
- cream: for combination and dry skins
- soap and water: use an unperfumed soap and rinse well.

Remember that some models like to wash their own faces.
   No matter which of the above methods is used, any
movement on the skin must be gentle. Heavy handling will
stretch the skin, cause broken capillaries, overstimulate the
sebaceous glands and damage the texture. Heavy handling can
also be uncomfortable for the client.
   Black skinned people should use plain mild soaps to clean
the face and body e.g. Neutrogena to cleanse the face. Toning
should be gentle and non-irritating. Use 25 per cent solution
of Witchhazel for dry skins and 75 per cent solution of
Witchhazel for oily skins. To moisturize use a low-oil formula
e.g. Neutrogena Moisture.
Before commencing cleansing, fully prepare yourself and your
client as described in Chapter 1.

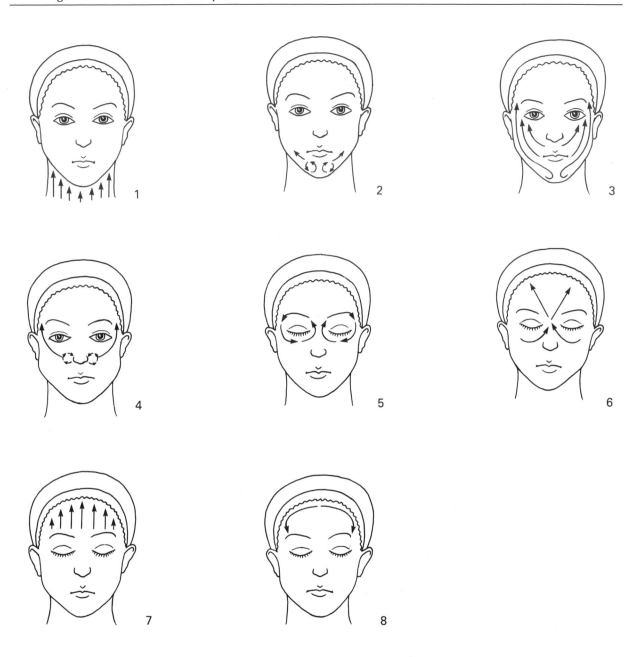

Figure 2.1 *Routine method for cleansing and make-up application*

The routine method

The step-by-step routine described below can be used to spread the cleanser over the face with your fingers. It can be repeated using damp cotton wool pads to remove the cleanser. It can be used again to apply astringent; to apply moisturizing lotion; and to apply foundation using small soft sponges.

First dot cream evenly over the face. Use your hands and finger tips in unison to spread the cleanser evenly over the face, producing a relaxing and logical flow of work as you progress up the face to finish at the temples. It is important to move smoothly over the skin and not drag it. Your movements must be gentle and even.

The numbers in the following sequence correspond to those on Figure 2.1:

1 Start on one side of the neck. Using a gentle stroking movement with one hand following the other, wipe upwards over the skin to the jaw-bone. Work to one side of the neck and then back to the other, finishing at the centre.
2 Using both hands so that they work in opposition and starting at the centre point of the chin, make little circles.
3 With both hands working in unison, wipe across the cheeks with a stroking movement from the chin to the temples, and then from the chin to the corner of each eye. Repeat these movements, working inwards towards the side of the nose.
4 When you reach the nose, use circular movements to work around the nostrils.
5 Make a gentle circular movement around the eyes. *Do not touch the eye make-up.* If no eye make-up is present, circle very gently over the eye area twice.
6 Using your right hand, and starting on the client's left side of the nose, stroke upwards, crossing the side and top of the nose and ending on the forehead. Repeat this gentle stroking action with your left hand over the client's right side of the nose. Repeat this four times.
7 Using upward stroking movements with one hand following the other, start at the centre of the forehead and work across from one side to the other.
8 Finish by pressing the temples at the same time, then remove your hands.

The removal of eye make-up and lipstick must be completed separately, after cleansing cream or liquid has been applied once.

Cleansing the eyes

Removal of eye make-up is difficult, as it is formulated to stay on. It is best to use proprietary eye make-up remover; this enables you to remove the make-up without rubbing the delicate eye area too much.

The procedure for cleansing the eyes is as follows:

1 Use cotton wool buds and eye make-up remover.
2 Hold the skin taut at the eyebrow.
3 Start under the eyebrow on the outside edge of the eye. Gently rotate the cotton bud down the eyelid as far as the lashes. Repeat, moving along towards the inner edge of the eye until eye shadow is removed.
4 Take a clean cotton bud with remover and rotate down over the lashes. Hold another cotton bud underneath the lashes, and cleanse the lashes well between the buds.
5 Wipe the eyelid with damp cotton wool, from the inside corner to the outside corner.
6 Repeat this routine on the other eye. Do *not* use the same cotton bud or damp cotton wool on the other eye.

Cleansing the lips

1 Prepare two damp cotton wool patters with a little cleansing cream or liquid.
2 Place one patter on each hand over and under the fingers, as shown in Figure 2.2.
3 Hold one corner of the mouth, and slide the other hand gently across the lips.
4 Repeat, using the other hand and clean patter.
5 Repeat using alternate hands until the lips are clean.

Now return to cleansing the whole face and removing the cleansing cream/lotion. Repeat these movements (Figure 2.1) until the cotton wool patters show clean.

Freshening and moisturizing

Use skin freshener, astringent or toner, which all have a similar effect.

On a patter of prepared cotton wool, go over sweat spots to cleanse and close the pores. Let the face dry. The purpose of this is to remove all traces of dirt and cleanser after cleansing.

Most skin fresheners have an alcohol base, which makes them efficient at getting rid of any oil left on the skin.

Figure 2.2 *Holding cotton wool patter*

However, with a sensitive skin it is best to dilute the freshener with a little water using a damp cotton wool patter, or to use an alcohol-free toner.

Apply barrier cream, or use lotion or moisturizer with a very sensitive skin. Allow a few minutes to absorb into the skin. Wipe off excess.

Allergies

In most cases it is the perfume that causes a reaction. Most cosmetics except the hypo-allergenic ranges contain small amounts of perfume to mask the smell of some of the ingredients. Another common allergen, lanolin, is also the most efficient skin softener.

Reactions vary. Some people develop a fine red rash which itches and burns at the same time. Others experience a visible swelling of the eyelids or lips; sometimes blisters develop. If the reaction is immediate, stop using the make-up and send the client to a doctor for treatment.

Sometimes it is not obvious what is causing the reaction. In many cases a cosmetic product is not to blame, even though all the signs point to it. An allergy can as easily be caused by the food you eat, or any stress you may feel. In all events it is best to check with a doctor or a dermatologist.

Basic make-up

Foundation

Apply foundation base thinly and evenly using a sponge. For dry skin, choose cream or cake foundation. For oily skin, choose lotion or aquacolour wet make-up. For combination skin, choose paint-stick or whatever you prefer (Figure 2.1).

Remember that for a production you must cover face, neck, ears and hands. Arms must also be covered if they will show when held above the head in costume.

Always apply a foundation colour two or three times darker than natural base skin colour. This allows for the fading of colour under strong lighting.

Powder

Powdering is very important because it sets the foundation, ensuring that your make-up stays in place for a long time.

Powder generously with a large powder puff or large brush,

or a clean, dry cotton wool ball. Always tell your model you are going to powder, and ask him/her to close the eyes and take a deep breath. Do not take too long; remember that he/she is holding his/her breath. You can always continue with the second breath.

When applying powder, put it on all over the face, including eyelids, lashes and lips, because it provides a good base for eye shadow, mascara and lipstick.

To set the powder, take a damp patter and with a rolling motion lightly travel over the face in a consistent line, pressing down so that the patter removes the excess powder and gives a matt finish to the foundation. Check around the eyes carefully. This also has a cooling effect on the face and stops that itchy feeling that loose powder can give.

Always ask you model to open and shut the eyes as you work around them.

Note: If you have used an aquacolour foundation you do not need to powder.

Eye make-up

Eye make-up should be applied at this stage. For dry skin, a cream base helps to avoid a crêpey look.

No matter what kind of eye make-up you use, remember that it is the way you use it that is important because fashions change. The key to a successful eye make-up is to experiment in a subtle way with colours (see Figure 7.4).

Eyelashes: mascara

Before you apply mascara, check that the lashes are completely dry and free of grease. The mascara should be stroked on and left to dry. Then a second coat should be applied. Do not clog the lashes. Place a patter under the lashes to avoid spraying mascara on the skin around the eyes.

Mascara comes as a cake, a cream and a waterproof liquid. As with all eye make-up it does not matter which kind you choose. If, however, your model is going swimming or has to cry you will find that the waterproof kind is best. See page 17 for eyelash tinting.

Eyebrows

Use an eyebrow pencil. Never draw long straight lines; instead use little feathered strokes that follow the natural growth of the hairs. Sometimes it may be necessary to tidy up and shape the eyebrows, but this is mainly for fashion work and should be done half an hour before the start of the make-up.

A small eyebrow comb is very useful for combing and shaping the eyebrows, and is also used for removing any excess powder left in bushy eyebrows.

See page 97 for eyebrow shaping.

Rouge, shaper, blusher

Blushers soften and minimize bad features (pushing them into the background). Look at the model's chin, jaw-bone, cheeks, cheek-bones and forehead, always in relation to the rest of the face. Decide on the features you want to tone down and those you want to emphasize.

Oval

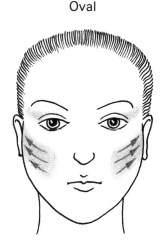

Square

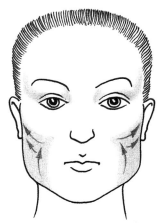

Heart-shaped

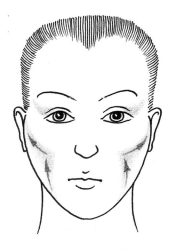

Round

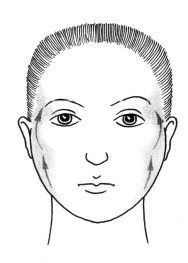

Figure 2.3 *Shadings for face shapes*

It is best to start shading with a blusher. Most professional make-up artists prefer the powder kind, applied with a large soft brush, because it is easy to blend with foundation.

Experiment on different face shapes. Once you know exactly what suits each face shape it will take only minutes to give the shading required. Typical shadings for the main types of face shape are shown in Figure 2.3.

Lips

A brush or pencil will be best for any outlining you wish to do.

You should bear several things in mind when you choose your colours: the shape of the lips, the colour of the foundation, the eye make-up and the colour scheme of the clothes or costume. The age and character should also be considered if the make-up is for a theatrical or media production (see page 95).

You should apply one coat of lipstick, blot the lips with tissue, and then apply another coat in order to make sure that it stays on.

Hair

Remove hair band and cap. Check the hairline is clean. Brush and comb hair. If the hair requires further hairdressing, or a wig or hair place is to be attached, do it at this point (see page 99).

Tidying

All dirty patters should be placed in a rubbish container, and all dirty brushes placed in a jar ready for cleaning. Bottle and jar tops should be wiped and replaced. The work area should be swept and generally tidied.

Removing basic make-up

Repeat the cleansing procedures thoroughly. The model can apply his/her own day make-up now. Alternatively you can apply it; use the same routine as before, but with the model's own make-up and colour range.

In some workplaces you may be required to wash the model's hair and style it in a manner suitable for going home or meeting the public.

Eyelash tinting

Permanent tinting saves the client having to use mascara every day. The tint will last as long as the lashes (about six weeks).

Eyelash tinting should not be performed on any client with a history of eye sensitivity or allergy or septic areas due to poor physical condition. A skin test should be performed 24–48 hours prior to tinting and if there is any redness, swelling or irritation that particular tint should not be used.

Method
Apply petroleum jelly in a line close to the lashes on the upper and lower eyelids (but not touching the roots) and place shaped pads of damp cotton wool under both eyes. Apply the tint to closed eyes with a fine brush or orange stick tipped with cotton wool. Do not touch the skin.

Test for colour on the first eye after 5–10 minutes. When the desired tone is reached remove both lower and upper pads together in a firm even movement from the outer corner to the inner corner. Remove any remaining tint with damp cotton wool pads.

Take great care not to get tint into the client's eyes. If this *does* happen the client should be given an eyebath of clean water to wash out the eye. If no eyebath is available the client should submerge their whole face in a basin of water and blink repeatedly.

Assessments

1 Practise the basic make-up sequence without referring to your notes.
2 Apply make-up for day wear to be used under strong lights on a stage. Always remember that light fades colour.
3 Apply make-up for evening wear to be used under strong lights on a stage.
4 Apply day make-up for use in television or under natural light.
5 Apply night make-up for a television play.

Practise on a male as well as a female – even on yourself. Remember to take photographs before and after application, as this will help you to understand what happens to make-up when the camera films it. Experiment using black and white film as well as colour.

These assessments will help you grow in confidence when working on a model's face.

---

3 Theatrical and media make-up: ageing

Make-up picture gallery

In order to be able to start theatrical make-up you need to collect pictures and photographs of people of all ages and nationalities which you can copy. For example:

- aged male
- aged female
- bald and balding heads
- beards and moustaches
- disfigurements – scars, cuts, bruises, grazes, black eyes
- hands – ageing
- necks and jawlines
- noses and eyes
- teeth and mouths
- happy faces
- sad faces
- characters from history and fiction
- skull
- clowns
- non-realistic
- animal faces
- faces and nationalities.

A good way to store these pictures is to use a large photograph album with see-through sheets to protect and hold them in place. If this is too expensive, make a scrapbook and paste in the pictures. It is important that, whatever way you choose to keep them, the pictures are well organized for instant reference.

Make-up file

Work sheets have already been mentioned in Chapter 1. It is important to prepare for make-up work and to keep good records of completed characters. Figures 3.1, 3.2 and 3.3 show a make-up file chart, a frontal pattern and a profile pattern. The patterns can be traced or copied for your work sheets.

1 Name   Date

2 Production

3 Character   Age

4	Base colour	
5	Highlights	
6	Shadow	
7	Powder/cake	
8	Rouge	
9	Lip colour	
10	Eye shadow	
11	Pencil	
12	Mascara/liner/false eyelashes	
14	Body make-up/hands/arms/legs	
13	False hair: wig/beard	
15	Hair: own	
16	Costume type/colour	

Draw in details:

A   B

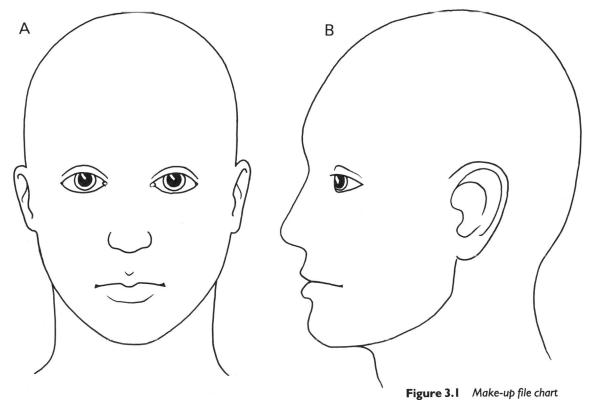

Figure 3.1 *Make-up file chart*

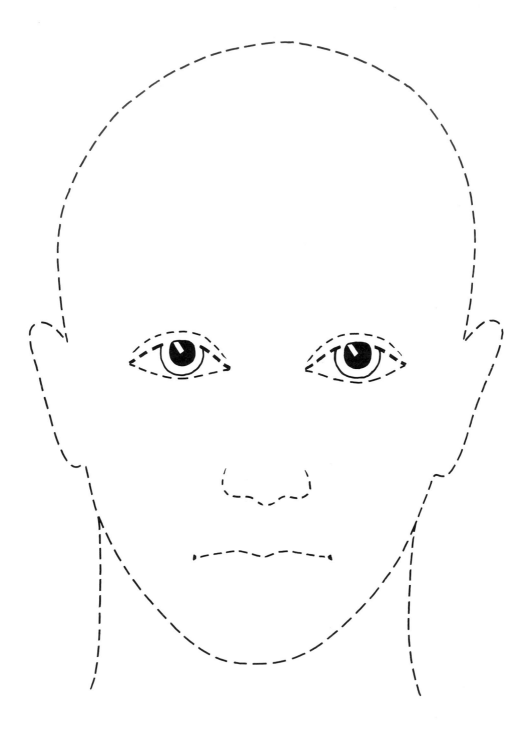

Figure 3.2   *Full face pattern*

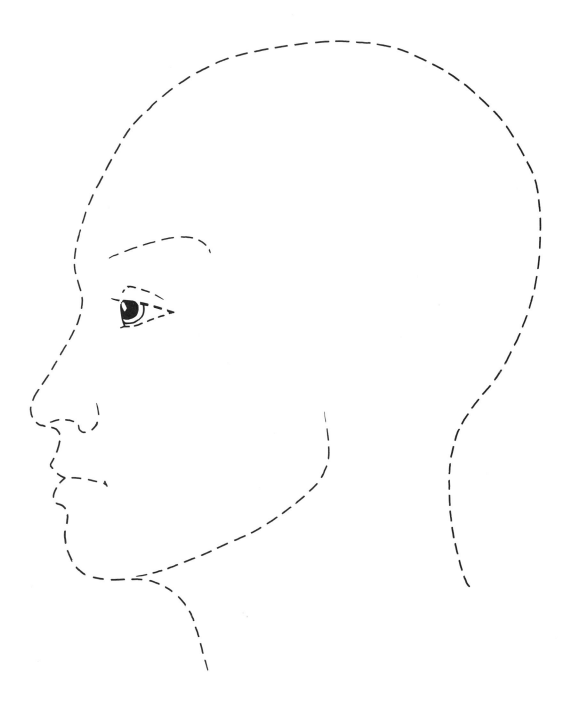

Figure 3.3 *Profile pattern*

Analysing the character

Using a work sheet, ask yourself the following questions:

1 Is the character male or female?
2 What age is the character?
3 What kind of life style, personality and physical appearance would this person have?
4 Is the character to be, for example, frail, ill or healthy?
5 What kind of complexion will the character require, for example sallow, translucent, weather beaten or over-indulgent?

The answers will help you to decide on your base make-up foundation colour.

An experimental make-up or a sketch showing what you have in mind is essential. If possible take a large photograph of the model before making the sketches. You can trace the model's face, then work on the drawing to show changes.

Structure of the face

You have completed your basic make-up and learned a basic work sequence. In order to start theatrical make-up you must understand how your face works.

In essence, the muscles in the face give the features, and the bones in the face give the shape. Look hard at the pictures of the skull in Figures 3.4 and 3.5. Note the prominences and depressions carefully.

Principles of ageing make-up

In this chapter we take ageing make-up of face and hands as a primary example of theatrical and media make-up work.

The art is to take an aged make-up through increasing years by starting at the eyes and working round the eye perimeter. Using the minimum of shading and highlighting you can age by five- and ten-year periods, gradually working down into the cheeks and neck area.

Make-up allows you to create an illusion of three dimensions by using the principles of light and shade. This is how it works:

1 Look at an object. What the eye sees depends on the light that is reflected from specific areas of that object to the eye.
2 The structure of your face will reflect light in a certain pattern, and this pattern of light reflection is what reveals the structure and gives you your individual look.
3 You can change the shape of your face with three-dimensional make-up using false noses etc. This new face will reflect different patterns of light and you will no longer look like you.
4 But if you paint on patterns of light to match those your face would reflect if you were actually to change its shape, you create an illusion. This makes people looking at your face believe they are seeing a different shape from your real one.

This becomes clearer as your practical expertise develops. This is the start of character make-up skills.

The two principal techniques of ageing make-up are:

Highlighting This adds colour by bringing forward and making features stand out. Therefore highlight prominent features first.

Shading This removes colour by taking back, causing receding of shape. Shading should be carefully applied and the edge always blended with the base make-up so that there are no

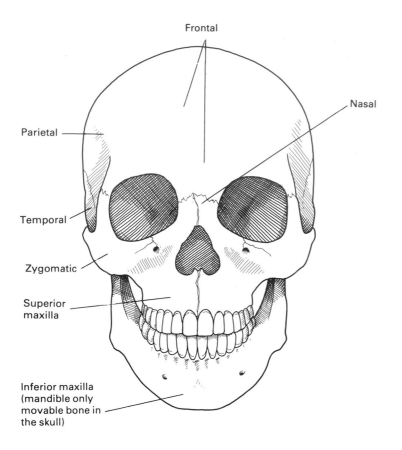

Frontal

Nasal

Parietal

Temporal

Zygomatic

Superior
maxilla

Inferior maxilla
(mandible only
movable bone in
the skull)

Figure 3.4 *The skull. The width and
shape of the face (oval, round, square) are
determined by the bone structure. The
skull gives attachment to muscles and
ligaments. The muscles of the face are
voluntary muscles i.e. controlled by will*

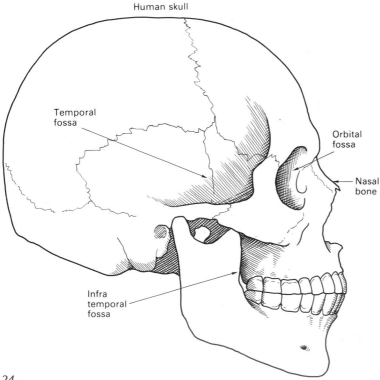

Human skull

Temporal
fossa

Orbital
fossa

Nasal
bone

Infra
temporal
fossa

Figure 3.5 *Skull prominences and
depressions*

hard lines. Note that if shading is too strong it can always be reduced by carefully stippling over with foundation colour.

Preparation and research

Now fill in your worksheet, carefully noting all the details. Be specific about features and colours.

If you are working on a production, talk to the actor or actress and the producer about the character. If it is from a play, read the book. If it is an historical character, look up biographies and examine photographs and paintings.

Ageing make-up for middle-aged male or female

Foundation

Apply the base colour (foundation) with a sponge. Choose a base colour about two tones darker than natural complexion colour. This is important because you need the depth of base colour for the highlight and shading to work. You should note at this point that you can use a model's own skin colour, if it is suitable for the type of character and production.

Very dark skinned people do not usually wear foundation. Sometimes a slightly lighter foundation is applied in order to make the black shadows work well. This is the only time you would use a cold shadow colour. Very dark skins may bleed through the base foundation, producing a chalky effect. It is best to use a camouflage base such as Covermark. Remember to cover neck and ears.

Highlights

Take a medium-size flat brush and load with a very pale complexion colour such as pale cream or ivory. Do not use white. Work with the diagrams.

Work as follows. The numbers correspond to those in Figure 3.6.

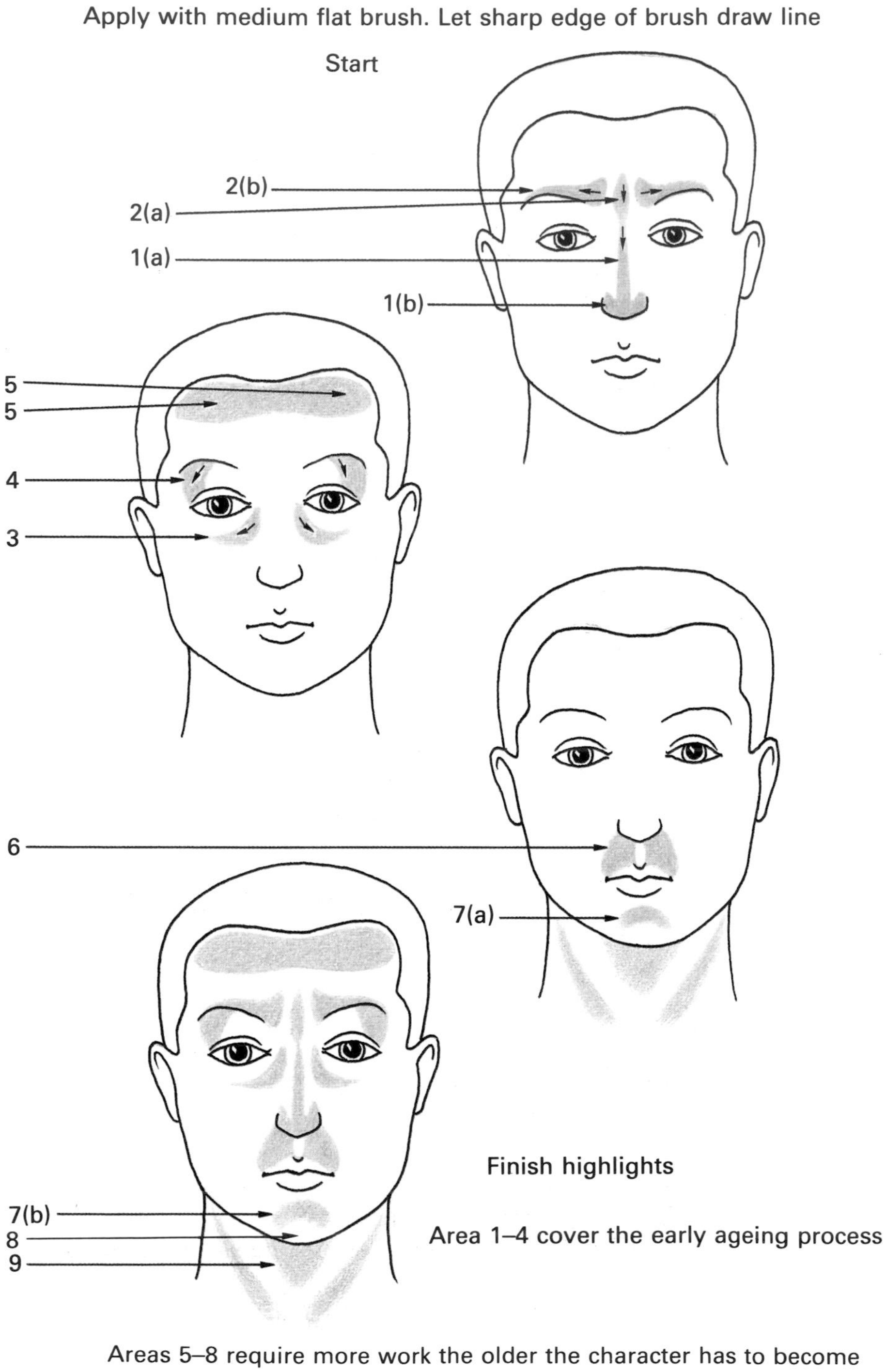

Apply with medium flat brush. Let sharp edge of brush draw line

Start

2(b)

2(a)

1(a)

1(b)

5
5

4

3

6

7(a)

Finish highlights

Area 1–4 cover the early ageing process

7(b)
8
9

Areas 5–8 require more work the older the character has to become

Figure 3.6 *Highlight areas for age make-up*

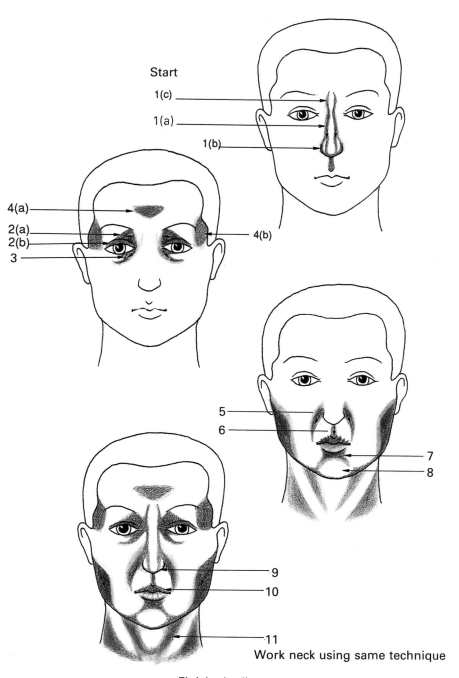

Start

1(c)

1(a)

1(b)

4(a)

2(a)
2(b)
3

4(b)

5
6
7
8

9
10
11

Work neck using same technique

Finish shading

Figure 3.7 *Shading areas for age make-up*

1 (a) Draw a line down the nose.
  (b) Highlight each nostril.
2 (a) Ask model to frown. Now paint the top soft parts of the frown only, not the crease.
  (b) Take highlight outwards along the top of the eyebrow. Let the highlight become softer and fade towards the end of the eyebrow.
3 Draw a loop under the eyes, following any natural pouch crease that may be indicated.
4 Draw a line from about the centre of the eyebrow to the outside corner of the eyelid (I call these eye curtains). Fill in this area softly and fade up to eyebrow. You may wish to highlight the eyelid at this time, but some people prefer it in shadow. This is an area to experiment with.
5 Move up to the forehead and place highlight along and below hairline and follow prominent skull areas.
6 Move to top of lip area under the nose. Draw a straight line using the smile crease, starting at the nostril. Do not take the line past the end of the mouth.
7 (a) Move to prominent chin area and draw a line.
  (b) Move brush to create a soft fade over the chin.

Now look at your model under a strong spotlight from some distance away. The model's skull structure should be more apparent and the fleshy areas should sag. Overall you should have the effect of age even if at this moment it is somewhat strong in effect.

8 If more ageing is required you may draw along the jawline with a wide brush and highlight.
9 Work on the neck using the same technique: see Figure 3.6.

Shading (shadows)

Take a new medium-size flat brush and load it with a dark crimson colour. Do not be put off by this colour. Clench your hand into a fist, look at the colour of the shadows in the creases, and remember that you are working two tones darker than natural colour. You will understand that the colour is right.
  Work as follows.

1 (a) Paint in the shadow area next to the nose.
  (b) Paint each side of the nose.
  (c) Take a very fine brush and draw in the furrow lines between the highlight areas.

2 (a) Paint in the eye sockets up to the eye curtain and highlight.

  (b) Paint the eyelids.

3 It is best to draw the shadow line above and parallel to the highlight line under the eyes.

4 (a) Depending on the age of the character, a little shadow may be added to the middle of the forehead.

  (b) Shadow may be applied to the temple areas. Always feel for the soft area of the skull for the correct position.

5 Draw a straight line above and parallel to the smile highlight area. Start at the nostril crease.

6 Shadow in the central area above the top lip.

7 Shadow in the central area below the bottom lip and up to the highlight line that begins the chin.

8 You can also shadow under the jaw along the jawline, but blend down into the neck carefully.

9 Place two shadows in the nostril holes. Use a clean brush.

10 Draw a line along the line of closed lips – quickly, because it tickles. You could extend this line slightly and use for making cracked lips.

Figures 3.6 and 3.7 summarize the highlight and shading. You will find at this point that the make-up is quite stark and unlifelike, although it may be acceptable for fantasy or horror make-up.

Blending

We now need to blend the highlights and shading very carefully. I will give you guidelines, but this is an area that you have to practise.

Use two small flat clean brushes, one for highlight and one for shading. Always blend highlight before shading if possible.

Never blend parallel lines, i.e. where the highlight line and the shading line run parallel with each other. For example, do not blend the following (numbers refer to Figure 3.8):

1 eye pouch area: highlight 3 and shade 3

2 smile crease area: highlight 6(a) and shade 5

3 eye curtain area: highlight 4 and shade 1(b)

4 chin area: highlight 7(a) and shade 7.

Always keep the lines clean and well defined.

The following are the blending areas. The more experienced you become, the less blending you will find you have to do.

When you have completed
the highlights and shading the
make-up should look like this

First follow direction of the arrows

Blend
Highlights

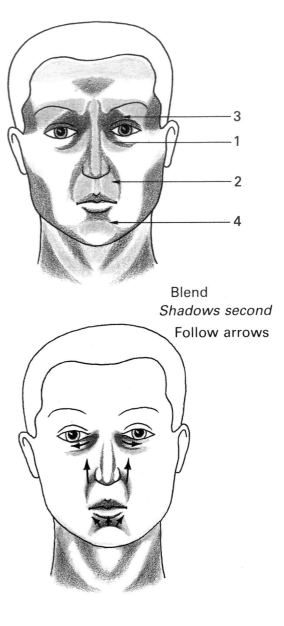

3

1

2

4

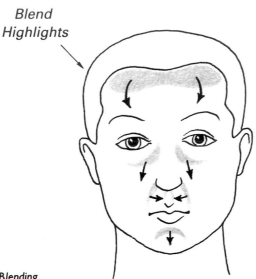

Figure 3.8 *Blending*

Blend
Shadows second

Follow arrows

Completed ageing make-up

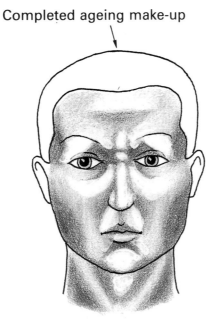

Figure 3.9 *Example of successful
ageing make-up*

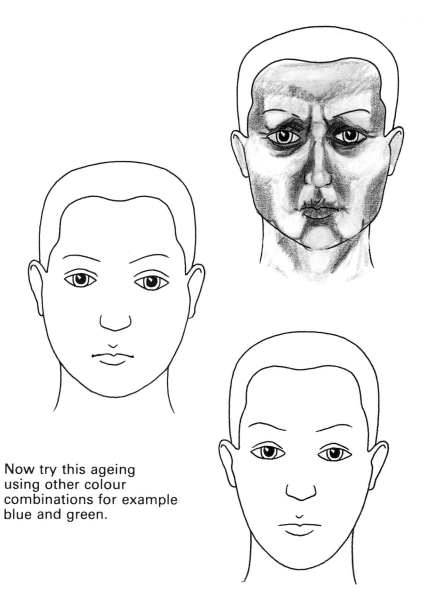

Now try this ageing using other colour combinations for example blue and green.

This is the time to stand well back and decide if any areas need to be deepened in shadow, e.g. by hollowing the cheekbones or deepening the eye sockets.

Figure 3.11 illustrates the results of blending.

Powdering

You powder now if you have been using cream or greasepaint.

Take a large powder puff and press translucent powder into the make-up. Remove excess powder with a powder brush. Set the powder with a damp patter, especially around the eye areas.

Reviewing the work

You now need to look at the make-up very carefully and consider different factors which could affect your next procedure:

1 Is this for the stage, to be seen at great distance and under very strong lighting?
2 Is this for the theatre in the round, to be seen quite close?
3 Is this for film or television, where the cameras are so good that they can pick up the smallest brush stroke out of key? Such work requires the highest accuracy and dedication to detail.

Whatever you decide about this make-up, you know you must practise make-up for the other areas.

The first time you complete this basic ageing make-up you will find that the results are quite harsh. Here are some remedies you could try:

1 If the make-up lacks colour and warmth, try adding some powder rouge with a brush to the shadow areas of the eyes, to the cheeks and (sparingly) to the nose to bring the work to life.
2 If the make-up has too much shadow and looks older than you wanted it, try stippling some base colour lightly over the shadow areas only, using a sponge (see next section).
3 If the make-up is too stark, try stippling a warmer base colour lightly over the complete face.

Stippling

Take a sponge that will give you the texture you require. Choose your colour and gently, sparingly, pat it on to the skin over the area requiring the stipple.

Be cautious. It is possible to flatten the make-up so much with stippling that you lose all the three-dimensional effect that you have built up.

Other finishes

Ageing make-up would not always finish with powdering or stippling.

If the character required was, for example, an elegant old lady, you would add her ordinary make-up to the ageing make-up, e.g. lipstick, eye shadow and rouge.

Figure 3.12 shows an example of successful ageing make-up.

Assessments

You can work on your own face or on a male or female model.

1 Design and apply a middle-age make-up for a character on television.
2 Design and apply an old-age make-up for a character from a film.
3 Design and apply 40-year-old make-up to a young person for the stage.
4 Select an idea from your project pictures.

Take photographs before and after make-up. Remember to fill in your work sheets in great detail before you start work. Keep your work sheets with your photographs. As discussed earlier, compile a reference work book in which you keep a record of all your work. This will be useful to show when looking for a job, and will be a reference for you if you are required to repeat work.

Ageing hands

There are several methods of ageing hands. The choice depends on the illusion you are trying to create. It also depends on what the actor or actress will have to do with their hands when acting.

Hands must, however, match the face.

Method I

You can put a dark foundation colour into the hands, then wipe off excess make-up using a tissue. Rub off prominent areas; this gives an instant effect of slightly older hands.

Remember to powder and set the make-up.

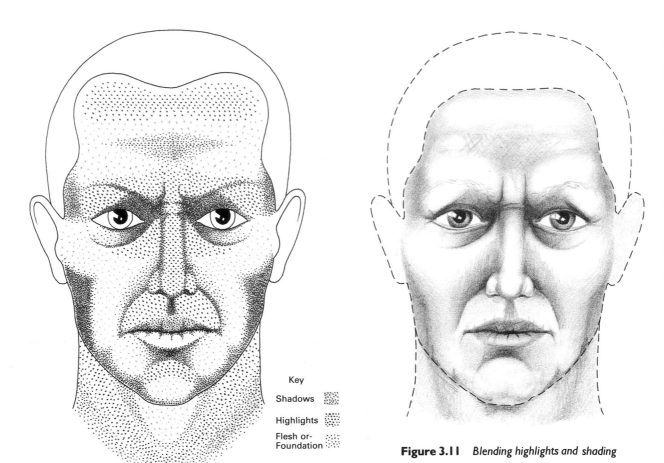

Key

Shadows

Highlights

Flesh or-
Foundation

Figure 3.10 *Summary of ageing highlights and shading*

Figure 3.11 *Blending highlights and shading*

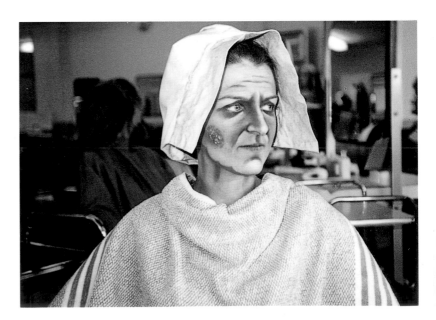

Figure 3.12 *Ageing 17-year-old model to 50 years using highlights and shading*

Method 2

You can model the hand with highlights and shadow in the same way as you did for the face and neck by using the same colours (Figure 3.13).

Foundation Rub foundation on to the hand with a sponge. Remember to use a foundation two or three times darker than the natural complexion colour. Remove excess foundation from the palms of the hands with tissue.

Apply foundation to top area of hand

Highlights

Centre of fingers and tops of all knuckles. Ask model to make a fist when applying the make-up

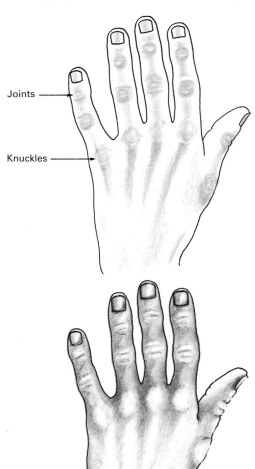

Shadows (dark crimson colour)

Shadow lightly on either side of the fingers and around the cuticle area. Shadow all the joints on one side mainly, but draw some thin line across them in the natural creases. Shadow all the knuckles on one side only.

Back of the hand: Draw blue/green veining on the skin and shadow one side only. You can stipple the skin with a brown foundation

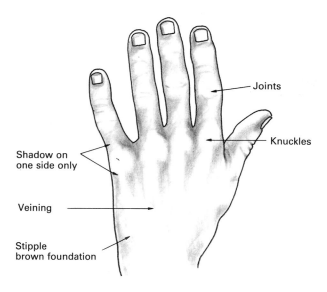

Note: Do not allow lines to form on the undersides of the fingers. Softly blend around the fingers

Figure 3.13 *Ageing hands*

Highlights Fingers: with a brush, draw highlights down the centre of each finger and thumb.
Back of hand: draw highlight down the bones of the hand.
Knuckles: highlight these prominent areas. It is easier to do this when a fist is made.

Shading Fingers: apply shading with a brush each side of the fingers and thumb.
Back of hand: shadow the bones of the hand on one side only (all shadows on the same side).
Knuckles: apply shading to all the joints but only on one side.

Extra effects Blue veining can be lightly drawn on with a blue brush or pencil. Make the veins slightly darker on one side only. Follow the veins on the hand. The colouring of veins can vary, so consider this. Remember to look at old people's hands during your research.

Brown spots are often found on ageing hands. They come in all sizes and can be dotted on the top of the hand. Freckles are usually smaller.

Powdering Powder front and back of hand. Remove excess with a powder brush. Coloured blending powder, white talcum or translucent powder may be used, depending on the effect you require. Set powder with a damp patter.

Stippling You can stipple the hand to give a texture. Use a darker or lighter foundation with a coarse textured sponge or a fine textured sponge depending on the character requirements.

Method 3

This method uses latex.
Various precautions must be taken. First, execute in a well-ventilated room. Second, use only latex that is manufactured for use on the skin. If you or your model feels any burning sensation when the latex is applied, remove it immediately.

It is best to protect the skin first with a barrier cream. Wipe excess off with a tissue and powder.

If the face or hands are hairy, it is again wise to protect them with barrier cream. If they are very hairy, like some male hands, it is best to cover them with some soluble spirit gum. Make sure all hairs are well covered. Wait until the spirit gum is dry. Now powder and remove excess powder with a damp patter.

To latex the hand for ageing, the steps are as follows:

1 Pull the skin tight by making a fist.
2 Work to Figure 3.14 in the order shown.
3 You can use your fingers also to apply latex.
4 Never use a brush because you will ruin it.
5 You may use a hair dryer to speed drying of the latex.
6 Powder and use a damp patter to set.
7 Now release the fist.
8 The skin should start to form wrinkles.
9 If deeper wrinkles are required, repeat the process.

Method 4

Make up the hand using your make-up skills as in method 2. Powder well, remove excess with patter. Now apply clear latex in the same way as in method 3. You should find this a much stronger ageing effect.

Method 5

Apply latex in the same way as method 3. This time, when it is dry and powdered and excess powder has been removed, apply rubber-mask greasepaint or cream make-up to make the ageing more apparent as in method 2.

Cleaning

To remove latex from the hands you carefully pull it off.

To remove the soluble spirit gum, just wash your hands with soap and water. If you have used non-soluble spirit gum you must remove it with a spirit gum remover or alcohol.

Rub hand cream into the hands when all make-up has been removed.

Assessments

1 Design a make-up for the hand of a corpse. Try to make it look as pale and translucent as possible.
2 Design a make-up for an ageing hand that belonged to a monster.
3 Design a make-up for a very old person.

Again keep a record of your work using work sheets and photographs in black and white and colour.

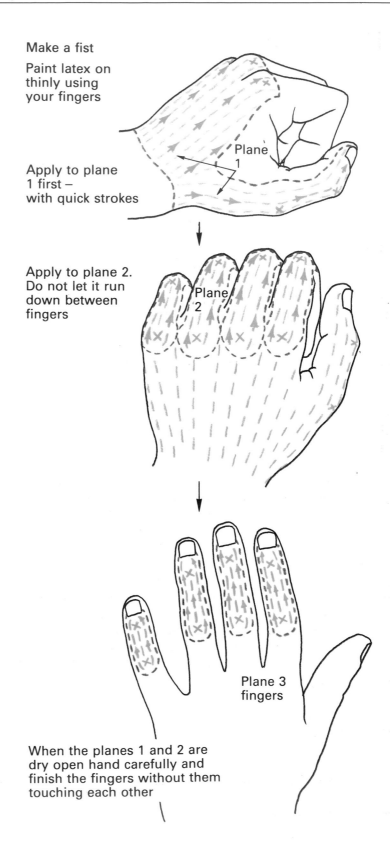

Make a fist

Paint latex on
thinly using
your fingers

Apply to plane
1 first –
with quick strokes

Plane
1

Apply to plane 2.
Do not let it run
down between
fingers

Plane
2

Plane 3
fingers

When the planes 1 and 2 are
dry open hand carefully and
finish the fingers without them
touching each other

Figure 3.14 *Ageing hand with latex*

4 Postiche work

'Postiche' is a French word used to describe any article of hair work. The article can be as small as a false eyelash or as large as a wig.

Hair structure

In order to work with hair to make postiche, we need to understand the external structure of a human hair (see Figure 4.1).

The hair grows out from the scalp of the head. The end where it leaves the skin is called the root. The end furthest from the scalp is called the point. The outside of a hair shaft is called the cuticle or outer layer. This grows in a scale-like manner with the scales lying towards the points of the hair.

Imagine a fish lying on its side: if you run your fingers from the head to the tail it will feel smooth, but if you run your fingers from the tail to the head it will feel rough. A healthy hair feels exactly the same: if you run your fingers from the point to the root of a hair it will feel rough, but if you run your fingers from the root to the point it will feel smooth.

When hair is attached to your scalp you know which end is which. If the hair is not tied before it is cut off, it is in danger of becoming mixed roots and points. If this is allowed to happen the hair will tangle, and if it is wetted it will mat together. This is because the cuticles are mixed up and they interlock with each other.

It is very important not to allow this to happen: no tangling or matting of the hair should occur. If mixed-up hair was made into a postiche, when worn it would tangle and be unwearable and therefore worthless.

Varieties of hair

Different kinds of hair are available (Figure 4.2):

● human hair: European, Asian

- animal hair: horse (legal postiche only), sheep (wool), yak (Tibetan ox), Angora goat (mohair)
- synthetic fibre (man-made substitutes): modacrylic, nylon, dynel.

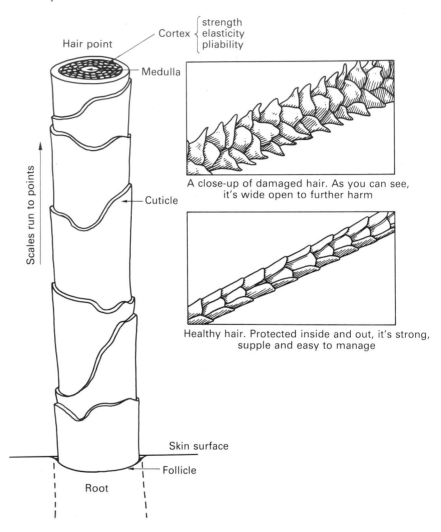

A close-up of damaged hair. As you can see, it's wide open to further harm

Healthy hair. Protected inside and out, it's strong, supple and easy to manage

Figure 4.1   *Hair structure*

Human hair

Human hair is available in a variety of colours and a range of textures. It is long lasting and hard wearing; usually the postiche foundation wears out first. It comes in various lengths, tightly bound with string at the root end, and may be straight or curly.

Hair is bought by weight (ounce or pound) according to type, length and colour. European hair is more expensive. It offers the widest range of natural colours and is the ideal texture for European hairstyles. Asian hair is less expensive.

Modern processing methods have succeeded in producing a wide range of colours and in refining the thick texture of Asian hair for European use. The hair now has good setting characteristics. It is good value, even if it does not last as long in good condition as virgin European hair.

Human hair is used for theatrical and media postiche, film and video work. It can always be styled – coloured, permed, bleached etc.

There are various possible sources of hair. Hairdressing students often come by enough hair to make facial postiche without spending money. Friends may keep their long hair and give it to you. Hairdressing salons often keep long hair to sell. Finally, hair may be purchased from commercial hairdressers, wholesalers and wigmakers.

Material	Source	Colour	Use
European hair (medium texture)	Germany, Scandinavia United Kingdom Spain France	Naturally blonds, some reddish Naturally dark Naturally brown and auburn	All postiche
Asian hair (coarse texture)	China, Japan, Indonesia	All colours, mostly artificial	All postiche, fashion wigs etc.
Fibre hair	Man-made modacrylics: Japanese Kanekalon, American Dynel	All colours	Fashion wigs, hair pieces
Nylon	Man-made	White, coloured	Display some theatrical fantasy work, some fashion wigs, practice pieces

Figure 4.2 *Sources and uses of hair and synthetic fibres*

Animal hair

Yak Yak hair is naturally black, grey or off-white, and is very coarse. It is particularly suitable for a stiff moustache or beard. It is sold by the ounce and is reasonably priced. It can be coloured.

Angora goat Mohair is very soft and is usually used for fantasy work. It colours beautifully but is very expensive.

Sheep's wool This is used as in crêpe rope (see Chapter 5). It can be used to make hair pads like bun rings, as well as for laid-on hair work such as beards and moustaches. You can buy it cheaply in most colours.

Beware of advertisements which say 100 per cent real hair, because it can be animal hair.

Synthetic fibre

Synthetic fibre hair can be permanently curled by using rollers and steam for one minute only. The permanent setting feature of this fibre is something real hair wigs cannot compete with, even though synthetic wigs need replacing frequently.

The simulated cuticle surface makes the fibre feel more natural and facilitates curling and back combing. The matt finish reflects light, like hair. The mixing of coloured fibres is very realistic, but in general the colours fade quickly in strong light. The fibres can be knotted or machine wefted.

Synthetic postiche is hot to wear. Some are used for the theatre but only the short modern styles.

Note that synthetic fibres are flame resistant but will melt easily. They may cause allergic reactions.

Synthetic fibre is sold by the ounce and is much cheaper than hair. It is available in various diameters and colours.

Cuttings

'Cuttings' is the name given to hair that has been tied and cut from the head. This hair is either cut by yourself or bought from a wholesaler (Figures 4.3 and 4.4).

Cuttings are usually in very clean condition. If they are not, they must be cleaned and disinfected as in the next section.

Combings

Combings are the hair which fall out of the scalp naturally when they have finished their life cycle. The normal life of a hair is from three to seven years. When long hair was fashionable it was the custom for women to save these combings and have them made into hair pieces in order to help build up their elaborate hairstyles. The ladies kept these combings in a combing bag. The roots and points of the hairs were mixed up.

Today 'combings' is the term used in the trade for hair that has mixed-up roots and points.

The method of unmixing the hair is called 'turning'. It is costly because it is time consuming, and it is little used today.

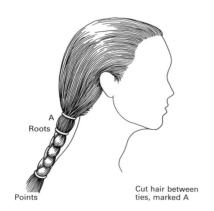

Figure 4.3 *Cuttings: wash and dry model's hair, tie roots, cut*

42

Figure 4.4 *Cuttings. The plait on the left is an example of cuttings: hair that has been tied first then cut from the head. The other sections of hair have been drawn off to length and tied at the root end: these large sections should be reduced to smaller sections for easy control and handling without waste*

Cleansing and disinfecting hair

Hair arrives in this country in hanks or in plaits. Because of infection it is essential that all hair is thoroughly washed in soap and water and disinfected either by heat or chemically. This is usually executed by the hair merchant before the hair is sold for general use. However, if you do have to prepare dirty hair, follow the instructions given below.

Chemical disinfectants are used to destroy bacteria. One of the most common types of bacteria carried by hair causes skin infection.

Disinfectants are used to destroy lice and nits; most products contain malathion. Check for nits with eggs present. Sometimes the hair still has dead eggs adhering to the hair shaft even though it may have been disinfected. Nits adhere very firmly to the hair shaft and are not easy to detach.

Where disinfectant or disinfestant is needed, use a proprietary brand. Note the following:

1 Read and follow the instructions carefully.
2 Label all bottles containing chemicals.
3 Store carefully.
4 Avoid contact with the skin.

Method of disinfecting the hair

1 Wear protective overall and gloves.
2 Tie the hair into small bundles (see later section on hair preparation).

3 Take care not to tangle the hair. Wash the hair in soap and water to remove any grease and dirt. Do not rub the hair.

4 Rinse in clear water.

5 Follow the manufacturer's instructions if using a proprietary brand of disinfectant. Alternatively, disinfect either by heat, or chemically with a reactant such as formaldehyde, hot carbonate of soda solution, denatured alcohol, or a solution of chlorhexidine.

6 Rinse the hair again carefully in clear water.

7 Use a hair conditioning agent to smooth the cuticles of the hair.

8 Place hair on to a flat towel to dry naturally in a warm place.

9 When the hair is dry, place it into a moth-proof container and store.

Method of disinfesting the hair

1 Wear protective overall and gloves.

2 Place the small bundles of hair in a pan with water, acetic acid and Gammexane (insecticide). Boil for about fifteen minutes.

3 Rinse in clear water.

4 Dry the hair.

5 If it is necessary to use a 'nitting machine', secure it firmly to the table in front of a hackle (a giant comb fixed to the table).

6 Draw the dry hair through the hackle and the nitting machine together. Draw from the roots to the points.

7 This removes the lice, nits and eggs, allowing them to drop from the hair into a tray.

8 The contents of the tray are then burned.

A fine-toothed comb can be used as an alternative if you do not have a nitting machine:

1 Hold the hair over a piece of paper. Draw the comb through the hair, allowing the infestation to drop on to the paper. Burn quickly afterwards.

2 Wet and condition the hair.

3 Dry the hair well.

4 Store in a moth-proof container.

When the work is complete, disinfect the nitting machine, hackle, fine combs, table and floor areas where you have been working, together with your overall and gloves.

Tools and materials for boardwork

Drawing brushes   One should fit on top of the other (Figure 4.5). These are used to hold the hair while you work and prevent wastage of the hair by keeping it under control, enabling you to draw out the longest hairs first.

Drawing mats   These are two mats of flat hardboard of identical size, fitted with L-shaped prongs designed to hold the hair in place (Figure 4.5). Place one mat on the table with the prongs facing away from you. Lay on the hair with the tied roots facing you. On top, place the second mat with the prongs facing away from you. The prongs hold the hair securely.

Net foundation

This is available from wigmakers or hairdressing wholesale merchants.

It comes in different varieties (see Figure 4.6). Finest flesh-coloured nylon lace is suitable for street wear, film, TV and photographic work. Heavier flesh-coloured nylon lace is suitable for the theatre.

Strong, stiff nylon net should be used by students first practising their knotting. Small pieces of net foundation are all you require to start with. You can use a stiff gauze to knot on, but it is only suitable for theatre use as the edge is difficult to disguise.

Knotting hook and holder

The knotting hook, which is sometimes called a ventilating needle, is a miniature fish-hook and is very sharp (Figures 4.6, 4.7).

Knotting hooks come in different sizes depending on the number of hairs you require in each knot. Size 00 is the finest and is used for finished edges, drawing only one hair at a time. Size 01 or 02 should be used for the main filling-in areas, drawing two or three hairs at a time. Larger hooks can be used where more hair is required without showing the edge.

Be careful not to wave the knotting hook around, or put the hand holding the hook up to your face. When you are not using the knotting hook, put it in a safe place so that you or another person cannot sit on it or place the hand on it. It is wise to put a cork from a bottle on the end of your knotting hook when it is not in use, or unscrew the hook and place it in a little box for safekeeping.

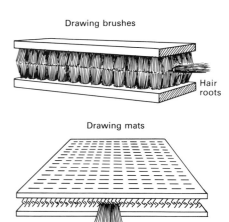

Drawing brushes

Hair roots

Drawing mats

Roots

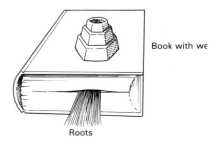

Book with we

Roots

Figure 4.5   *Holding hair*

Figure 4.6 *Boardwork tools and materials*
1 *Wire*
2 *Beeswax*
3 *Bottle of spirit gum*
4 *Finger shield*
5 *Small hammer*
6 *Spatula*
7 *Knotting hooks and holder*
8 *Small postiche comb*
9 *Covered watch spring*
10 *T postiche pin*
11 *Jockey*
12 *Postiche clip*
13 *Scissors*
14 *Straight postiche pins: used for setting on malleable blocks*
15 *Block points: used for foundation work on wooden blocks*
16 *Vegetable net*
17 *Fine theatrical net: sometimes called nylon lace*
18 *Tape: for blocking up lace front postiche and setting*

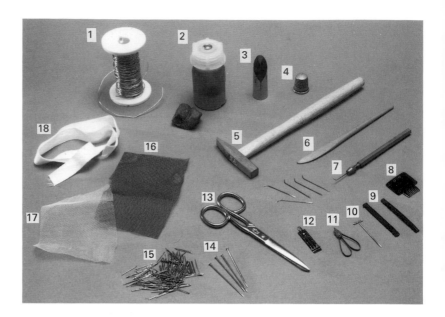

Because the hook is barbed, to remove it from the skin it must be forced around and up through the skin again. This can be done after unscrewing the hook from its holder. You must never pull at it because that would cause more damage. If you show care in using this small tool, this will not happen.

Blocks

These are available from wigmakers or hairdressing wholesale merchants.

Wooden block This is a head-shaped solid block. Wooden blocks are available in different sizes and are mostly used for making wigs. They are expensive but last a lifetime; however, other blocks can be used which are less costly.

Malleable block This is a soft block which is head-shaped and covered with canvas. It also comes in various sizes. It is used mainly for dressing and setting postiche.

Beard block This can be soft canvas or hard wood. Both are chin-shaped.

Plaster cast of head or chin

Plastic face and head This often comes with practice hair moulded into a scalp which fits on to the plastic head. Hairdressing students usually require one.

Ceramic head   This is mainly used for making bald caps.

Polystyrene block   This is either full head or just the crown. It is the cheapest type of block you can buy.

Availability   You can pick up polystyrene blocks at Oxfam shops and jumble sales. Sometimes you can find the wood and malleable blocks in antique shops. You need to collect as many as you can, as they are always useful.

Various blocks are shown in Figures 4.7 and 4.8.

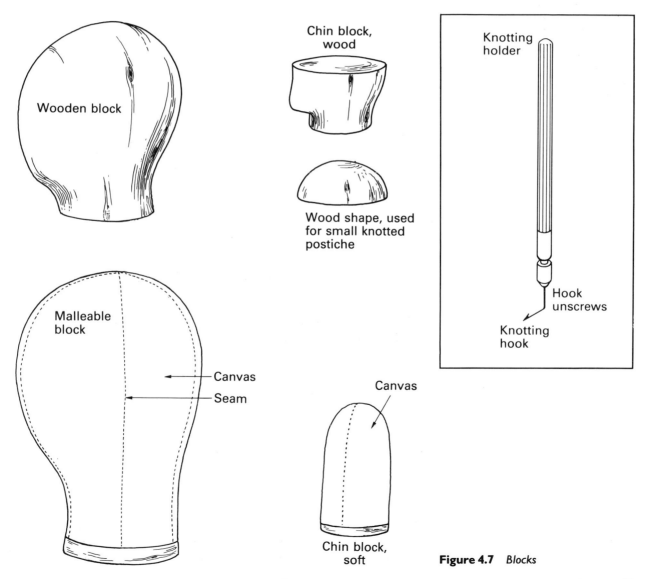

Wooden block

Chin block, wood

Wood shape, used for small knotted postiche

Knotting holder

Hook unscrews

Knotting hook

Malleable block

Canvas
Seam

Canvas

Chin block, soft

Figure 4.7   *Blocks*

Figure 4.8 *Malleable block shown on block holder. This block holder is a table size: floor-standing block holders can be purchased*

Hair preparation

Drawing off

This means separating the longest hairs from the shortest (Figure 4.9). You need to do this only when your cuttings are very tapered (e.g. if you have cut and tied hair from a model's head). It enables you to get maximum use from the hair without too much waste.

Place the tapered hair into the drawing mats with the points facing you. Place the second mat on top of the hair to hold firm. Now draw off the hairs that protrude the farthest with your index finger and thumb.

When you have repeated this once or twice, place this hair on one side (you must remember which way round you put it down because you are redrawing off the points).

After a while you will have separated the different lengths (A–E in Figure 4.9). Tie the root ends again.

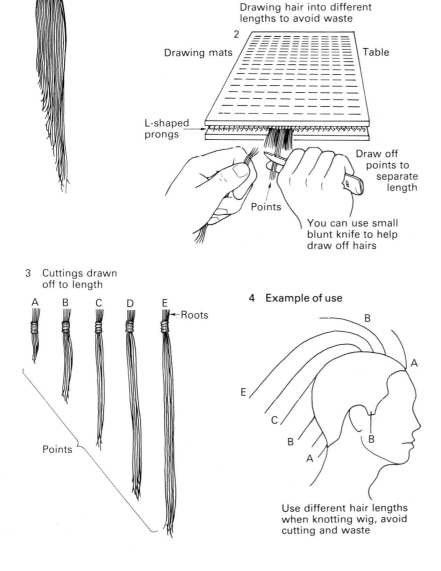

1 Cuttings with taper, e.g. pony tail cut from the head

Drawing hair into different lengths to avoid waste

2

Drawing mats

Table

L-shaped prongs

Draw off points to separate length

Points

You can use small blunt knife to help draw off hairs

3 Cuttings drawn off to length

A B C D E

←Roots

Points

4 Example of use

B

A

E

C

B

B

A

Use different hair lengths when knotting wig, avoid cutting and waste

Figure 4.9 *Drawing off hair*

Preparation of the hair (cuttings)

If you buy hair it will arrive in a large bunch, tied securely at the roots and middle.

You must now prepare small cotton ties in order to divide the hair into small workable sections. Take some thread and spread your arms wide. Take this length and fold several times until the folded thread is about 10 cm long. Now cut the loops top and bottom. You should have several ties. Repeat this as many times as required.

Prepare the hair as follows (numbers correspond to those on Figure 4.10):

1 Place the large bunch of hair on the table with the roots away from you.
2 Take large hairdressing scissors and carefully cut through the thread holding the hair together. Place the scissors into the hair in the same direction that the hair lies, so as not to cut the hair.
3 Spread out the cut thread and carefully remove from behind the bunch of hair by holding the root end firmly and lifting the hair up.
4 Place the bunch of hair down on the table again. Hold the roots in your left hand, and with your right hand divide a small section of hair off from the main body from one side. Hold the main bunch still, and at the same time draw the small section of hair from the main bunch with your hand. Do not do this too quickly or you may cause static electricity.
5 When the small section of hair is clear of the main bunch, tie the roots with one of the prepared ties. This section should be the thickness of a pencil.
6 Continue working in this careful way until you have prepared all the hair into small workable sections. This prevents wastage of hair.

If the hair that you have bought is very long, you can tie the small section in the middle as well, then cut the section in half above the middle tie (Figure 4.11).

The preparation takes a long time but it is worth doing in order to save time and money in your next exercises. If you have a great deal of hair prepared, it is best to make smaller groups of the sections of hair and fold them into sheets of paper. Then store in a tin or sealed polythene bags.

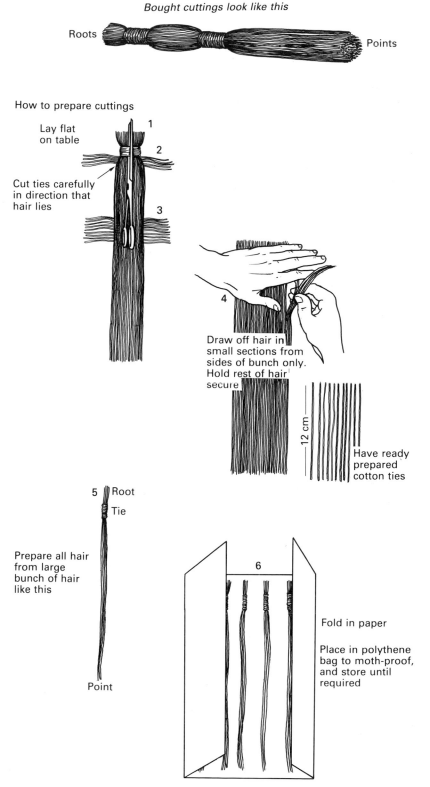

Bought cuttings look like this

Roots   Points

How to prepare cuttings

Lay flat
on table

1

2

Cut ties carefully
in direction that
hair lies

3

4

Draw off hair in
small sections from
sides of bunch only.
Hold rest of hair
secure

12 cm

Have ready
prepared
cotton ties

5   Root

Tie

Prepare all hair
from large
bunch of hair
like this

6

Fold in paper

Place in polythene
bag to moth-proof,
and store until
required

Point

Figure 4.10 *Preparation of cuttings*

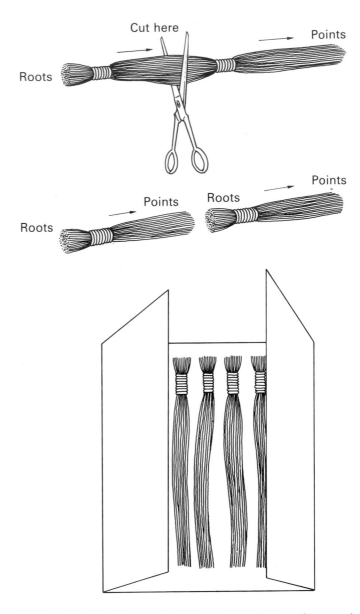

Figure 4.11 *Cutting long hair*

To avoid waste, break hair down into smaller sections and store folded in paper in airtight tin or polythene bag

5 Crimping and curling hair

Crimping hair permanently: crêpe rope

Crêpe rope is used in laid-on hair work, mostly for crowd make-up effects for film and the theatre. It is used for moustache, beard and sideburns, beard stubble and eyebrows. It is quick to use for one-off productions, and is cheap.

Crêpe rope is also used for making shaped hair pads. Hair is dressed over these pads to create bulk and a different hairstyle. The actor/actress may not have enough hair for the style required, but may not wish to wear a wig (e.g. bun ring) in a character part (see page 62).

You can buy sheep's wool crêpe rope in various colours, which is made in the same way. It is cheaper than hair crêpe rope. You could collect your own sheep's wool, but make sure it is well disinfected and disinfested (see Chapter 4) before you use it.

Crêpe rope can also be used instead of end papers when perming. It can be used to make cheap Afro wigs and clown wigs. It is not suitable for film or television close-ups.

Tools required

Two clamps, for use on a table.
Two weaving poles, one straight and one shaped.
Hammer, nail.
Pair of scissors.
Two folded pieces of paper the thickness of a finger.
Ball of smooth string.
Pair of drawing mats/brushes.
Hair to work with: can be combings.
Hairdressing clip.

How to set up weaving frame

The weaving frame is shown in Figures 5.1 and 5.2.

1 Take the ball of string and measure off two equal lengths. The quick way to do this is to stretch out your arms

sideways and measure three widths before cutting the string. Do this twice.

2 Take the first length of string and tie the end to the middle of one finger of paper. Repeat with the second length.

3 Take a shaped weaving pole and place first piece of paper plus string into top shade. Now hold paper still but wind the spring around the pole very tightly. When you reach the end of the string, tuck it behind the paper edge to hold it while you repeat this exercise with the second string.

4 You will repeat this with the second string in the shape below the first one. Make sure you wind both springs the same way. If you hold the shaped pole in your left hand, holding the end that fits into the clamp, wind the string away from you around the pole with your right hand.

5 Take the straight pole and hammer in the nail in position, as in Figure 5.1.

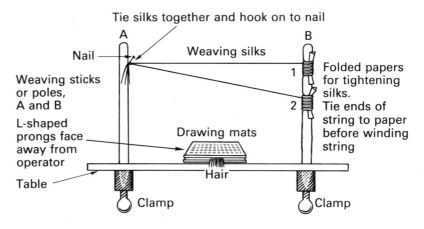

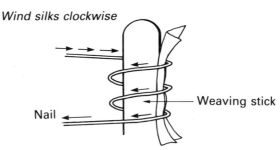

Both sections must be wound the same way

Figure 5.1 *Setting up a weaving frame for crepe*

6 Screw clamps to the table about 45 cm apart.

7 Take the pole with the nail and place it on the left-hand side.

8 Take the shaped pole and place it on the right-hand side.

9 Unwind the two ends of the strings and make two knots with the strings together. The knots need to be 2–3 cm apart.

10 Place the strings on to the nail between the two knots.

11 Tighten the tension of the strings by turning the papers. This makes weaving much easier.

12 If the poles slip in the clamps, wet some paper and wrap it around the bottom of the poles, then push them back into the clamps.

Figure 5.2 *Setting up weaving frame for crêpe*

Weaving the crêpe rope

1 Place hair into the mats or drawing brushes. The amount of hair you take depends on the thickness and length of the hair and the amount of crêpe you require.

2 Make a starting knot (Figure 5.3).

3 Proceed to weave the length you require. Join in new lengths by twisting the ends together (Figure 5.3). You may need to weave several colours separately if you want to mix them later.

4 You may find a hairdressing clip of some assistance in holding the hair when taking a new section of hair (in the trade this is called a jockey: see Chapter 6).

5 Continue doing crêpe weft until all the hair is used up, winding the weft around the left-hand pole as you proceed. This in turn releases more string from the right-hand pole.

6 When finished, cut the top string and tie it tightly to the bottom string at the end of the weft. Then cut the bottom string.

7 Place this weft in a pan and cover with soft water. Boil for 30 minutes or more. Lift out and allow to drain.

8 Leave to dry thoroughly.
9 When it is dry, store it in moth-proof containers. Leave it on strings until required.

You can make crêpe weft with cuttings or combings as long as the hair is not shorter than 15 cm.

Examples of crêpe hair and its use are shown in Figure 5.4.

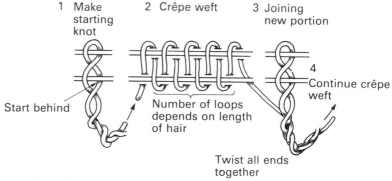

Take equal portions of hair each time:
small portions give tight crimp
large portions give loose crimp

1 Make starting knot   2 Crêpe weft   3 Joining new portion

4 Continue crêpe weft

Start behind

Number of loops depends on length of hair

Twist all ends together

1 and 2 ends joining

2 and 3 ends joining

5 *Push hair up tightly as you weave: rope starts to look like a plait*

6 When you pull hair off rope it looks like this

Figure 5.3 *Make a crêpe rope*

Figure 5.4 *Examples of crêpe hair and its use. A bun ring is on the left-hand side. The third piece of hair along the back shows that only half the length of the hair has been crêped: this is useful if fullness is required without using too much hair, e.g. for increasing the weight of a beard. The end of the white crêpe rope has been opened and pulled out to show its possible fullness: this crêpe rope is made of sheep's wool*

Laid-on facial crêpe hair work

Equipment required

Spirit gum.
Various colours of crêpe rope (wool or hair).
Scissors.
Drawing mats.
Tail comb and orange stick.
Surgical spirit or spirit gum remover.
Electric iron.
Gown and face towel.
Face powder.

Planning the work

Determine the shape and colours of the facial hair required.
Be aware of the natural line of hair growth.

Work to a picture or drawing and prepare a work sheet: see Figures 3.1–3.3.

Preparation of crêpe hair

1 Cut the crêpe rope into the lengths that you require for your beard or moustache.
2 Cut the string holding the plaited crêpe. Pull the strings away, holding one end carefully.
3 Wet the hair slightly, then iron it out to straighten it. If a steam iron is not used, place the hair under a damp towel.

4 After the hair is dry, carefully comb it with a wide-toothed comb. You can also tease it with your fingers.

5 You should now mix your colours if required. Lay one length over the other and gradually comb and tease together.

6 Alternatively, take a little of one colour then a little of another and keep mixing them together with your fingers. You need to experiment with this.

Applying crêpe hair for a beard

Using the numbered sequence shown in Figure 5.5, start at the chin and work towards the neck edge. Complete the chin and work up the sides of the face.

To apply the hair, put spirit gum on to the skin a little at a time. Wait for it to go tacky, then press on a little crêpe. Build up the beard like this. Use the clean edge of a tool to press each layer on to the face.

Keep dark hair underneath the chin, lighter hair on top of the chin. The lightest hair should be on the edges so that it will fade into the skin. The sides of the beard usually have less hair.

Trim the beard to shape using a dressing comb and scissors (see section to follow). When the beard is dry, test it by gently pulling. This will remove stray hairs and also make sure it is secure enough to wear on stage (this method is not usually used for television). When the beard is satisfactory, spray it with hair lacquer.

Moustache

Apply crêpe in the same way. Using the sequence continuation shown in Figure 5.5, start from the outside edge and work towards the centre. If a full moustache is required you can wax or gel the ends.

Stubble effect

You can use left-over bits of crêpe rope for this. Cut the hair into very short pieces and then paint the area to be covered with matt spirit gum. Leave it to go tacky. Take an old thickish brush, place it into the stubble bits, then dab them on to the face.

You could also place the stubble on a dry cloth, then press it on to the face. Whatever you use will become sticky.

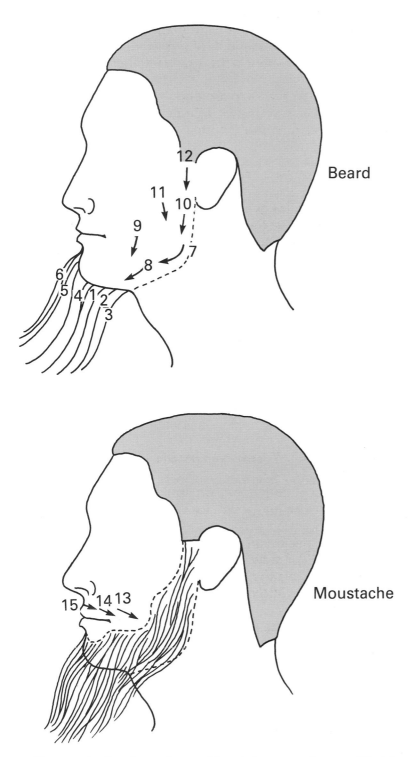

Beard

Moustache

Cut end of crêpe that will stick on to face with bias, so that more ends of hair stick on to skin

Figure 5.5 *Applying crêpe hair to make full beard and moustache*

Eyebrows

Crêpe eyebrows can be made by sticking crêpe on to the skin above the eyebrows, then combing the crêpe down over or into the real eyebrows. Note that you must not get spirit gum on to the real eyebrows; you should first block out the eyebrows.

Removal of laid-on hair work

1 Protect model with plastic gown.
2 Place towel around neck.
3 Protect eyes with damp patters.
4 Brush spirit gum remover along top edge of moustache. Allow it to go smooth, then pull off the moustache gently. Continue to brush remover along the top edge of the beard, then down and under the chin. Remove hair as you go: never pull until it comes away easily.
5 Clean off the skin with remover.
6 Wash off the remover.
7 Then cleanse the skin with cream.
8 If the skin is inflamed, a very cold towel pressed to the face is beneficial.
9 If removing crêpe from eyebrows, be very careful not to get remover into the eyes.

Shaping and trimming beard or moustache

You require: one cutting or dressing comb, one pair of hairdressing scissors, a gown to cover the model, and a mirror.

First you must decide on the shape and style you require. If you have a picture or drawing, it will help. Look into the mirror at the model's beard and moustache. Look at your picture and decide what you have to cut or trim to make it look the same shape.

Bring the comb to the line of the shape you want with your left hand. Now take your scissors in your right hand and cut along the top of the comb in that line. Repeat the same line on the other side. Take and cut a little hair at a time, keeping an eye on both sides of the face. Always lift the comb a little when in the right position. Check the shape from the side view.

This make take a little practice, but will be safe if you always keep the comb behind the scissors and in front of your model's skin.

If you are applying crêpe hair over cream or greasepaint, powder the make-up very well first.

Assessments

1 Carry out an ageing make-up with a full laid-on beard and moustache. Mix some hair for this: see section on mixing later in this chapter. First complete a work sheet and take a photograph. When the work is complete, take a photograph of the full beard.
2 Cut down beard to medium size. Take a photograph.
3 Cut down to stubble. Take a photograph.

Crêpe hair pads

These are pads of frizzed hair that can be made into various shapes (Figure 5.6). The shapes can be useful in transforming a model's hair into a character hairstyle very quickly and effectively. Small hair pieces can be attached to these hair pads and the hair dressed over the pads.

If a large shape is required, frames of light wire can be constructed which are covered with net. This net is impregnated with the crêpe hair ready for the model's hair to cover.

Actors like to use their own hair. When this is practical, such pads are invaluable. Always keep some made up in your work box.

To make a bun ring

1 Set up weaving frame as for making crêpe rope.
2 Take a crêpe rope of the required colour.
3 Cut the strings and pull out the crêpe hair to release it from the strings.
4 Start to weave pad weft on to the weaving frame (part 1 of Figure 5.7). Use the width of the crêpe hair. You can use the crêpe rope that you have bought or some that you have made yourself. I prefer the sheep's wool crêpe for this work.
5 Weave 10 cm. The bun ring diameter will be 10 cm when teased out. Weave tightly to get as much hair in as possible.

6 Make sure each end of the weft is well tied off. You cut the
top string first, then tie into the second string. Leave a long
length of string at each end. You need these strings to tie
ends A and B together to make a bun ring (see parts 2 and 3
of Figure 5.7).

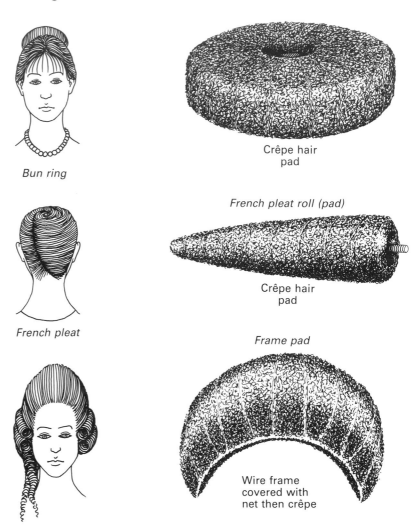

Bun ring

Crêpe hair
pad

French pleat roll (pad)

French pleat

Crêpe hair
pad

Frame pad

Wire frame
covered with
net then crêpe

Figure 5.6 *Crêpe hair pads and frames*

To make a French pleat pad

Weave straight as in part 2 of Figure 5.7. Do the same work as
in parts 3 and 4 but do not tie the ends together. First tease out
the hair, turning it round and round. Tease the hair together to
avoid gaps. Make it large and fluffy, then start to prod the hair
back on itself with a large hair pin. Keep the shape in mind and
turn all the time. Note: do not prod the pad in one place for
too long or you will make a dent.

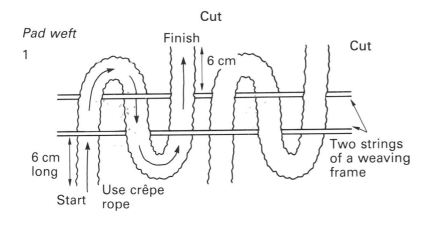

Pad weft

1

Cut

Finish

Cut

6 cm

6 cm long

Start Use crêpe rope

Two strings of a weaving frame

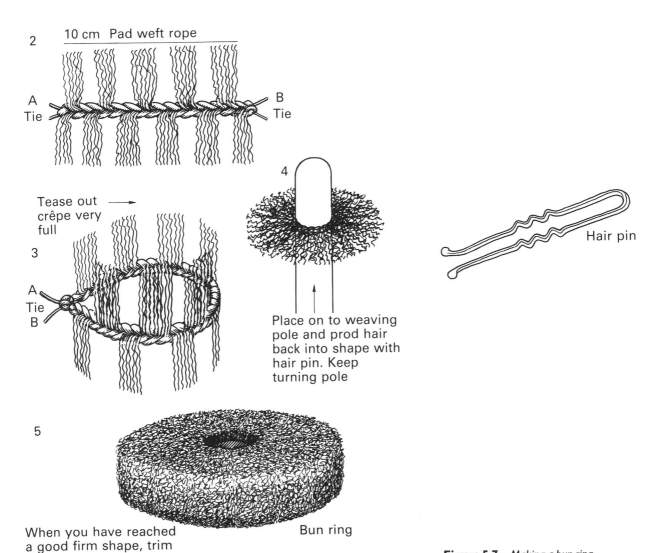

2   10 cm Pad weft rope

A Tie   B Tie

Tease out crêpe very full

3

A Tie B

4

Place on to weaving pole and prod hair back into shape with hair pin. Keep turning pole

Hair pin

5

When you have reached a good firm shape, trim with scissors

Bun ring

Figure 5.7 *Making a bun ring*

Figure 5.8 *Hairstyles using crêpe pads*

To help produce the correct shape, you need to cut the pad to the right size when the crêpe has firmed up. Be careful not to cut the strings.

Hairstyles using pads

These pads are easy to attach to the head with hairgrips and hair pins, which will easily pass into the pads. Figure 5.8 shows hairstyles which would have used such hair pads, ranging from 300 BC to AD 1978.

Other applications of crêpe hair

Crêpe hair can also be knotted on to a fine net foundation to make a knotted beard or moustache (see Chapter 12).

Crêpe hair can also be used when creating animal masks, as well as latex-based masks with beards and moustaches.

Assessment

Prepare a work sheet for a chosen historical hairstyle using a hair pad. Make the pad and dress out into the hairstyle. Photograph before and after.

Curling hair permanently: *frisure forcée*

Frisure forcée is used for curling or waving hair 15 cm and over in length. The permanently curled hair will then be used in postiche work.

Tools required

Jigger, called the third hand. This is used to hold things, enabling you to have both hands free to work (see Figure 5.9). It is not necessary to have a jigger if you can have two holes made in a table instead. Whether you have a jigger or two holes, the important thing is to have a loop of string under which you can place the hair on the table. The foot holds the other loop of the string near the floor.

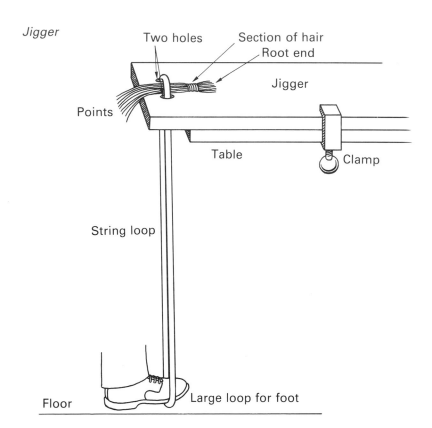

Bigoudis (curlers)

Made of wood,
glass,
hard plastic
that does not
distort when
boiled. Various sizes

Jigger

Two holes Section of hair
Root end
Points
Jigger
Table
Clamp
String loop
Floor Large loop for foot

Figure 5.9 *Jigger and bigoudis*

Bigoudi curlers: select size according to degree of curl required (see Figure 5.9).
Bowl of water with a little acetic acid; end papers.
Ties of cotton 30 cm long. Prepare and tie small sections of hair at root end for curling.
Pan of soft water for boiling prepared bigoudis.
Towel to place bigoudis on to collect excess water before drying.

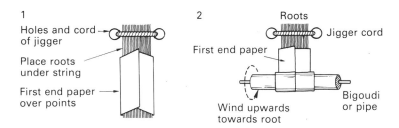

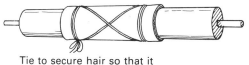

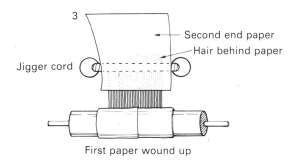

Figure 5.10 *Winding hair for* frisure forcée

Method of curling hair

1 Decide on size of curl required and choose your bigoudis accordingly.
2 Secure jigger to table. Check loop of string is comfortable for your foot.
3 Take prepared section of hair and dampen it in bowl of water.
4 Place root end of hair under loop on the table (Figure 5.10, part 1). Hold in position with foot in loop on the floor.
5 Take end paper and fold around the points of the hair.
6 Take bigoudi and wind end paper plus hair around the bigoudi (part 2 of figure).
7 When you reach the loop of string, take another end paper and fold around the roots (part 3 of figure).
8 Relax foot on string loop at the same time. Remove and wind second end paper around bigoudi.
9 You should not be able to see any hair (part 4 of figure). It should all be enclosed in the tissue paper around the middle of the bigoudi. If the hair is long, you may need another end paper.
10 Place back under the table loop and hold with foot in floor loop.

11 Take a long tie and secure ends of end papers by tying in a figure eight. This must secure the hair inside the end papers so that it will not come out during the boiling (part 4 of figure).
12 Place in pan of soft water and boil for 30 minutes.
13 Dry in airing cupboard or postiche oven.
14 When the hair is dry, remove end papers carefully.
15 Remember the hair that comes off the bigoudi first is the root end. If the tie has become loose, retie roots now.
16 Place curls in a moth-proof container.

To avoid faults:

- Use even tension when winding the hair.
- Tie threads securely.
- Wind hair evenly. Avoid fish-hook ends.
- Avoid winding too much hair around each bigoudi.

Mixing hair

It is often necessary to mix hair to match a particular shade. There are three reasons for mixing hair.

- colour match – by mixing two or more colours together and to produce grey hair by adding white
- taper – by mixing various lengths together.
- texture – by mixing coarse and fine hair together.

Tools required

Hackle with brush (Figure 5.11).
Ties for the hair.
Paper to keep the hackle clean.
Workroom sample from client for matching hair colour.
Drawing mats to hold assessed proportions of hair.

A hackle is a giant comb for combing and disentangling the hair. It must be screwed or clamped to a work table before use. Always store at low level: it is dangerous if dropped. If it is permanently fixed to a work table, it must be fitted with a safety cover.

Method of mixing

1 Hackle must be secured to table (Figure 5.11).
2 Push large piece of strong paper down on to hackle prongs with large brush, taking care not to catch fingers on the prongs. This paper keeps the hackle clean and enables a quick change by lifting paper out of hackle using a tail comb.
3 Take two shades of hair first and practise mixing (Figure 5.12).
4 Place hair into hackle.
5 Take and hold both colours together. Now comb repeatedly through the prongs. Keep twisting the hair to enable mixing.
6 Check the middle of the section mixed for colour match. If it is right, leave it.
7 If not, place the hair in the hackle again, place brush on top and draw off longest hair first. After a while this should separate the hair again, avoiding waste.
8 By adding small quantities which overlap it is easy to remove hair if necessary.
9 Mixing is done by pulling the hair through the hackle and kneading the hair at the same time.
10 When the hair is mixed, tie it at the root end.
11 Store the hair in a moth-proof container.

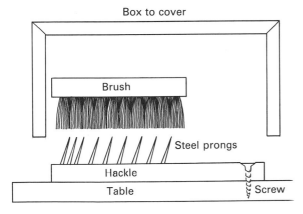

Figure 5.11 *Hackle with brush*

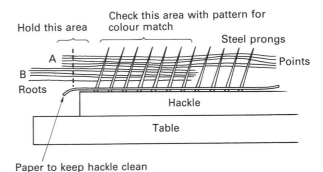

A Light shade of hair
B Darker shade of hair

Figure 5.12 *Mixing hair: this layout enables you to separate the sections if the mixing does not colour match the pattern, avoiding waste of hair*

6 Woven hair additions and extensions

In order to pass the City and Guilds examination in wigmaking you must make two examples of woven hair postiche:

- two-stem switch
- diamond mesh.

They are both useful hair pieces and can be made to any size (Figure 6.1). The measurements given here will be to the basic requirements given by the City and Guilds examining board.

Figure 6.1 *Two-stem switch and diamond mesh*

Weaving and wefts

Weaving is the method of securing hair on to strands of silk, on a weaving frame, so that the hair is fastened to the silk by its root end. The root ends must be kept short, no longer than 2 cm. Weft is a length of this weaving. Different methods of weaving produce different effects.

All wefts begin with a starting knot and end with a finishing knot (Figure 6.2). To make a starting knot, the points are taken from left to right in front of the roots and placed over the bottom silk from the front to the back of that silk. To make a finishing knot, the root end is taken from the right to the left in front of the points and placed over the bottom silk from the front to the back of that silk.

The wefts that you will use are as follows (Figures 6.2, 6.3):

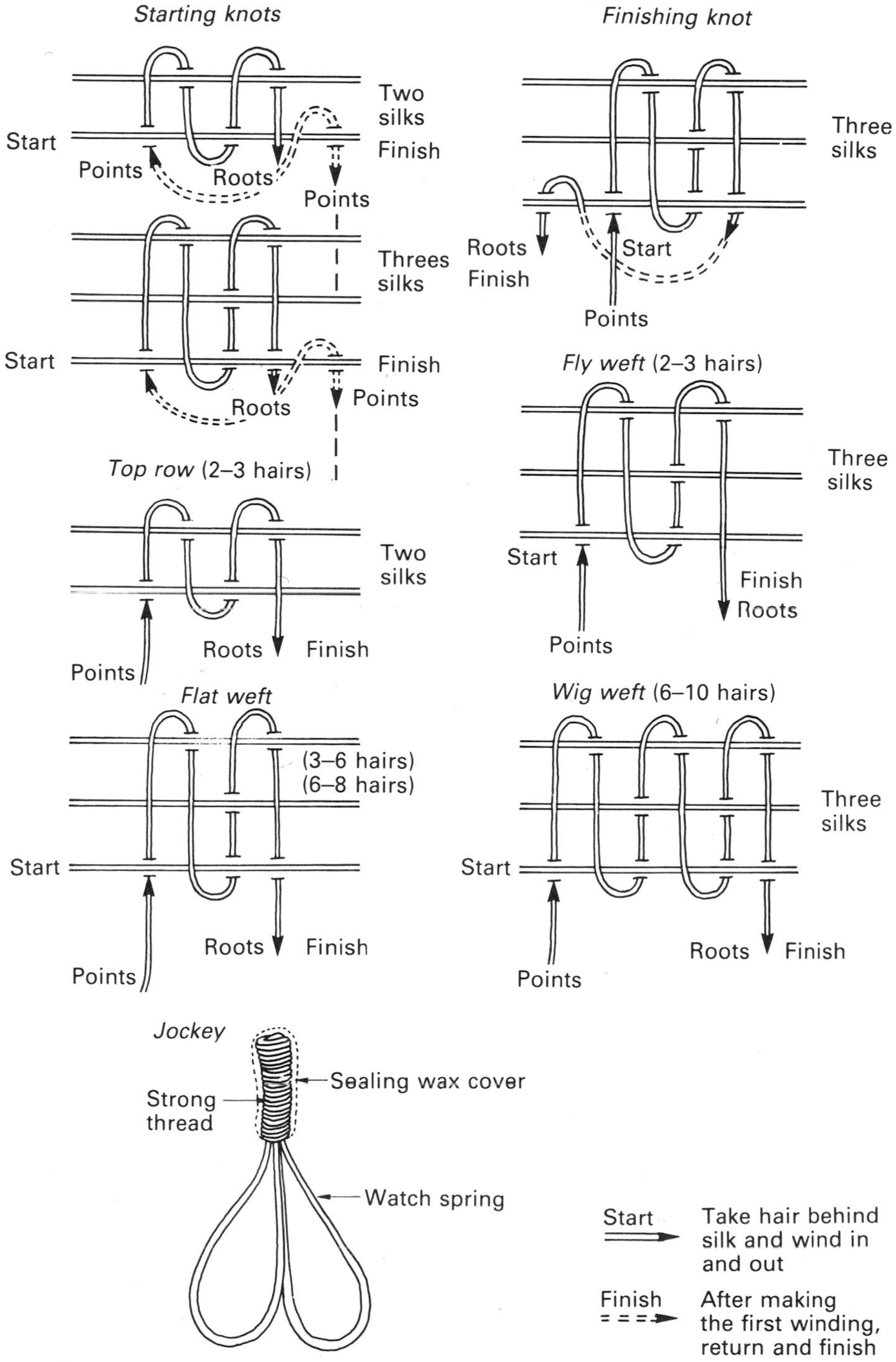

Figure 6.2 *Wefts*

Figure 6.4 *Creoled hair before and after plaiting to show fullness of hair*

Figure 6.3 *Sample wefts*

Top row This is woven using 2–4 hairs at a time on two silks. It is used for the first part of some wefts. It should be a very fine weft as it comes to the top of the work when it is sewn up, giving a neat finish to the completed postiche.

Fly weft This is the same as top row except that it is woven on three silks.

Flat weft or once-in weaving This is woven using 4–8 hairs at a time on three silks. It forms the body of most wefts.

Wig weft or twice-in weaving This is woven using 10–20 hairs at a time on three silks. It covers distance more quickly than flat weft. Used for diamond mesh clusters, wefted wigs and crowd theatrical wigs.

During weaving the roots can jump out of the silks, especially if you are keeping them very short. To help hold the weft you can use a hairdressing clip or make yourself a 'jockey' – so called because it rides the weaving silks.

To make a jockey, take two pieces of watch spring about 5 cm in length (Figure 6.2). Bend one to form a loop and bind with strong thread; do likewise to the other. Tie both loops together firmly. Melt a little sealing wax on to the tied end of the spring, moulding it to cover both the string binding and the spring ends.

Another aid can be the use of beeswax. Just run it along the weaving silks. Rub your fingers up and down the silks to smooth the beeswax before commencing weaving.

Switches

A switch is a tail of hair mounted on a thin cord. It is sewn in this way to give the illusion that the hair used is longer than it really is.

Switches are classified according to the number of stems, for example:

- one-stem switch: pony tail
- two-stem switch: coiled chignon
- three-stem switch: plait.

Creoling

Hair used for making switches can be permanently creoled beforehand in order to give the switch a little bulk. Take sections of the hair and plait it down to the points. Secure the points. Boil these plaits in a pan of soft water for 20 minutes. Remove and dry on a towel (Figure 6.4).

Note that the amount of crimp from the creoling depends on the size of the plait.

If you require bulk on the inside of the switch only, keep some hair smooth and straight for the outside of the switch (compare switches in Figure 6.4).

Making a two-stem switch

Weaving

Set up your weaving frame as in Figure 6.5.

Your hair needs to be prepared into two equal portions, one portion for each stem. However, you also need a smaller portion of longer hair, with which you will start off both the stems. Place the hair you are going to use into the drawing mats (see Chapter 4).

Start the first stem (Figure 6.6):

1 Draw off two hairs and complete a two-silk starting knot.
2 Complete 4 cm of top row.
3 Add the third weaving silk now. Take the end of the silk over to the nail. Unhook the loop and tie all three silks together, *twice*, still leaving a loop to place back onto the nail.
4 Continue to weave 20 cm of flat weft. When you start on the new silk, keep it loose until you have completed three wefts; then tighten all the silks together.

5 Finish with a three-string finishing knot.
6 Wind the poles so that you now have a gap of about 10 cm from the end of the first stem weft. Do *not* cut down.

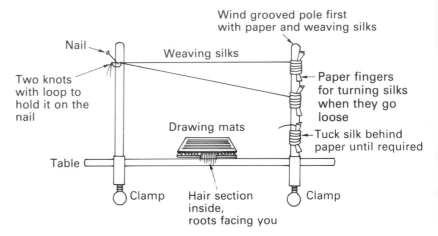

Figure 6.5 *Weaving frame set up for two-stem switch*

Go on to the second stem:

1 Make a starting knot (three-string).
2 Make 2 cm of fly weft (three-string).
3 Continue to weave 18 cm of flat weft.
4 Make a finishing knot.

Unwind all the weft and leave it on the frame. Cover the weft with tissue paper. Heat some pinching irons. They should be warm only: test on paper. Press the weft carefully (Figure 6.7).
    Cut down at the finishing knot end.

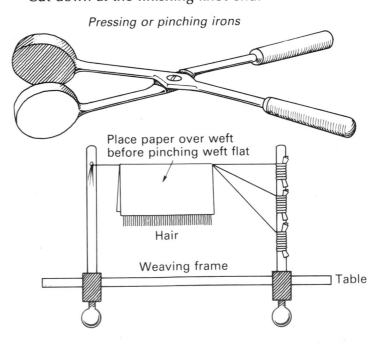

Figure 6.7 *Pressing the weft*

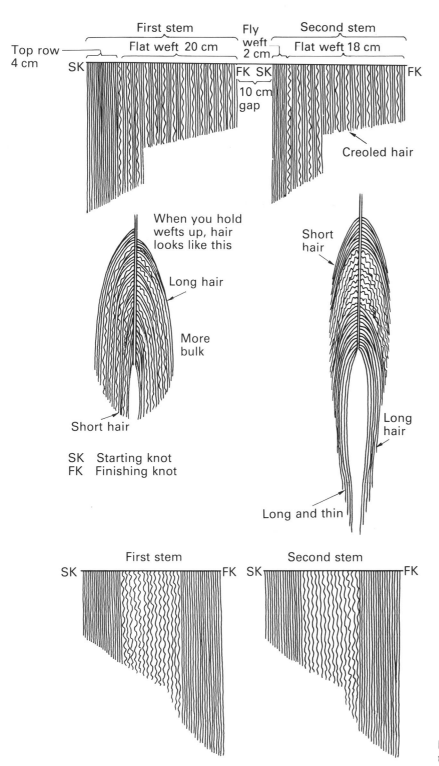

Top row 4 cm

First stem
Flat weft 20 cm

Fly weft 2 cm

Second stem
Flat weft 18 cm

SK
FK SK
10 cm gap
FK

Creoled hair

When you hold wefts up, hair looks like this

Long hair

More bulk

Short hair

Short hair

Long hair

Long and thin

SK   Starting knot
FK   Finishing knot

First stem

Second stem

SK   FK   SK   FK

Figure 6.6   *Two methods for weaving a two-stem switch, showing distribution of weft and use of hair lengths*

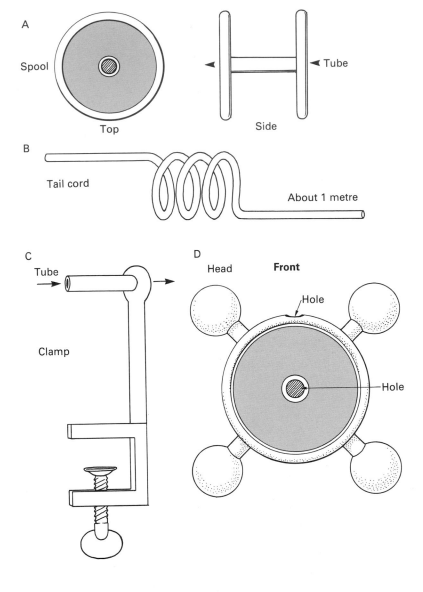

Figure 6.8 *Parts of a winding machine*

Sewing up the switch

Equipment needed:

- needle
- cotton/silk to match hair
- beeswax
- three pins
- winding machine (twisting machine) (see Figure 6.8)
- tail cord.

1   Tie end of tail cord on to middle of tube on spool.
Wind cord around centre until most of length has been wound
on (like a cotton reel)

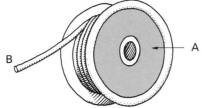

2   Thread this cord through outer edge hole of head
3   Now drop spool into middle of head

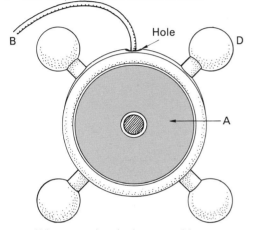

When completed, place on table

4   Fix clamp firmly to table. Take head and spool
and place on to clamp, passing clamp tube
through middle of head

5   Thread cord through back of head so that it
comes out at front of clamp tube

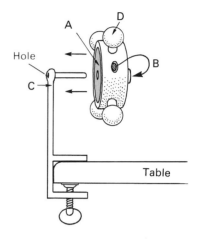

Figure 6.9   *Setting up a winding machine (letters A–D refer to Figure 6.8)*

Set up your winding machine (Figures 6.8–6.10). You may be able to hire this tool from a college if you are working at home. Prepare the sewing silks; pass through the beeswax.
Proceed as follows:

1 Take the second stem first. Starting from the finishing knot end, attach by sewing this end to the end of the tail cord. Allow enough tail cord for you to hold.
2 Twist the head of the winding machine anticlockwise. This in turn twists the cord and in so doing takes the weft, with you guiding it, up the cord. Proceed slowly and spiral the weft closely together like a spiral staircase. Stitch the weft at intervals as you advance.
3 When you reach the starting knot, fasten off securely.
4 Cut the tail cord 2 cm above the weft.
5 Take the first stem second. Starting from the finishing knot, proceed as for 1 and 2 above *but* only as far as the top row weft.
6 Take the second stem and sew this to the tail cord just above the weft of the first stem (Figure 6.11, part 1).

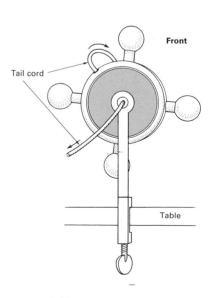

Figure 6.10   *Winding machine set up*

77

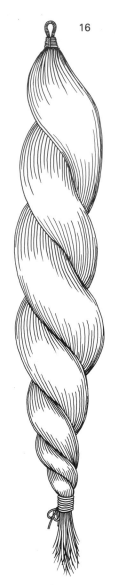

Figure 6.12 *Dressing a two-stem switch. Coil the stems first then dress into a chignon*

7 Take the top row weft that is loose and *without sewing* wind it around the joining stems up the cord. Where this finishes, place a small pin and unwind the top row.

8 Measure off enough tail cord to make a silk loop above this pin.

9 Place a second pin at the place you measured off (part 2 of figure).

10 Prepare sewing silk to match the colour of the hair and run it round and round the tail cord so that it is completely smooth and covered. Secure silk when you reach second pin, which you remove.

11 Cut the tail cord above second pin position.

12 Fold back to form a silk loop and sew (part 3 of figure).

13 Tie the silk loop to the winding machine tail cord (part 4 of figure).

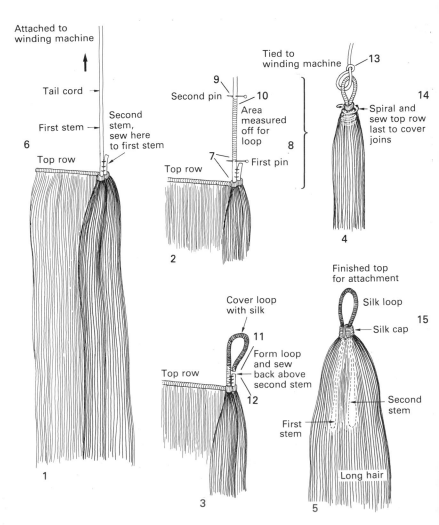

Figure 6.11 *Sewing up a two-stem switch*

14 Take the top row weft and spiral and sew this up over the joins until you reach the starting knot. Secure and cut thread (part 5 of figure).

15 To finish, take a new piece of sewing silk and wind this smoothly around the top of the weft and silk loop. We call this finish a silk cap. It must be small and neat.

16 You can now pin the switch to a malleable block and set it by coiling the two stems and then dress into a chignon (Figure 6.12). Note that the measurements given will only make a small chignon (doll size).

17 For attachment to the head, use hair grips or a small pipe cleaner.

Making a diamond mesh chignon

A unique feature of this hair piece is that the middle weaving string is replaced by a fine wire. This gives strength to the weft, enabling it to be made into various shapes.

The diamond mesh can be made with short, medium or long hair, depending on its required use. The minimum length of weft required for this postiche is 100 cm.

Preparation

Draw a pattern of the size of chignon required. Place the pattern on a malleable block. Take fine string (or wool) and follow the pattern around, starting from the middle. Pin with small pins as you proceed (Figure 6.13).

The length of string that you use to complete the design will give you the required length of weft (see Figure 6.13).

Weaving

The entire weft is usually woven in fine wig weft, although flat weft has become popular. To make a circular base 9 cm in diameter will require about 112 cm of weft.

Set up the weaving frame and proceed as follows:

1 Measure off 150 cm of wire. Wind this clockwise on to the middle groove section.

2 Measure off two 150 cm lengths of weaving silk. Wind these independently with paper for turning on to the other remaining grooves. Make sure all three are wound the same way.

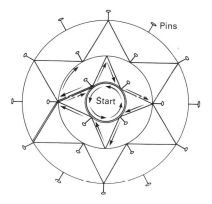

Figure 6.13 *Designing a diamond mesh chignon – use string to find the length you require*

79

3 Take the free end of the wire and wind it around the nail.

4 Take the free ends of the weaving silks and make two knots to form a loop. Hook this on to the nail.

5 Place hair into drawing mats.

6 Commence with a starting knot (Figure 6.2).

7 Weave 30 cm of fine flat weft (Figure 6.2).

8 Weave 82 cm of fine wig weft (Figure 6.2). This gives the required total of 112 cm of weft.

9 Finish with one finishing knot (Figure 6.2).

10 Open weft out to press flat.

11 Cut down, using pliers for the wire.

12 Turn in 1 cm of wire at each end of the weft so that the weaving cannot slip or come loose. Cover the wire with over-sewing to match the colour of the weft.

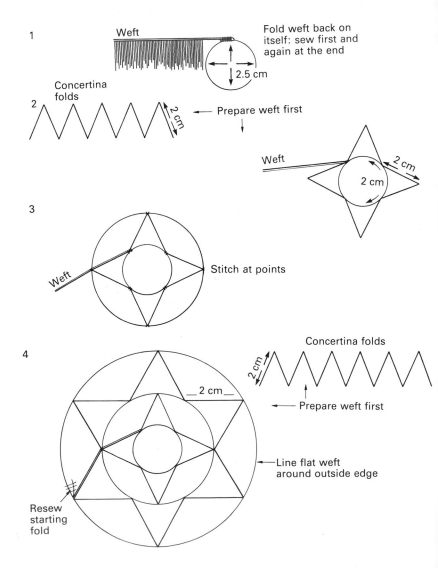

Figure 6.14 *Sewing up a round diamond mesh chignon*

Sewing up the mesh

Measure off the first fine flat weft and mark by tying some white cotton. This will indicate when sewing up that you have almost reached the weft that goes round the outside edge.

The weaving must be measured accurately when sewing into shape, and care must be taken to see that the roots are enclosed on the inside of the postiche.

The weft is sewn up as follows (Figure 6.14):

1 Form a circle, starting from the finishing knot end of the weft. The circle is 2.5 cm in diameter. Sew this (part 1 of figure).
2 Next, bend and concertina the weft to form four equal points which go around the circle. Use measurements given. Sew at each point that touches the circle (part 2 of figure).
3 Make a second circle with the weft around these four points and sew to the points (part 3 of figure).
4 Make six concertina points of equal size and sew around the circle (part 4 of figure).
5 Sew the remaining weft to form a third circle around these points, stitching at the points to complete the circular base (part 4 of figure).
6 You can sew a small comb on the side of the circle for attachment.
7 Block up on a malleable block and dress into desired style.
8 When dressed out this postiche can be attached to the head using hair grips and hair pins (Figure 6.15).

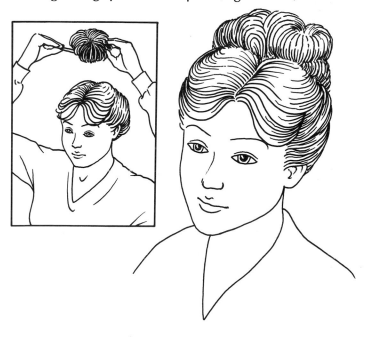

Figure 6.15 *Attaching a diamond mesh chignon of short curly hair*

Assessments

1 Describe a switch.
2 What types of weaving are used in the making of a switch?
3 What is the name of the machine used to sew up a switch?
4 How is the hair divided for a switch?
5 Which stem do you sew up first?
6 When do you attach this stem to the other stem?
7 When do you sew the top row up?
8 How do you make the loop?
9 What do we call the finished covering between the weft and the loop?
10 Give an example of how to wear this postiche.
11 What are the benefits of a wired mesh?
12 What are the wefts called that you used to make a diamond mesh?
13 How do you ensure that your measurements are correct for your pattern?
14 How do you secure the ends of the weft before you start to sew up the circle?
15 Explain how to sew up the diamond mesh in a circle.
16 Design one other shape that you could use.
17 How would you attach this hair piece to the head?

Hair extensions

I have included hair extensions for you to try because they are becoming very popular. They are not as yet included in any examination syllabus, but I am sure they will be. Here are some ideas for you to try now that you have learned to weave hair into weft.

You can buy long cheap Asian hair in a wide range of European colours as well as dark Asian colour. You can buy long cheaper synthetic fibre, which also comes in a wide range of colours and curl. Which to buy will be easier to determine after you have finished reading this section.

Extensions are required to add length of hair to short hairstyles. They are popular with clients who have very curly or Afro textured hair. Actors and actresses who do not want to wear a wig will often use extensions to give the illusion of a head of long hair. Extensions are cooler to wear than a wig. They are also cheaper than hiring a wig for several weeks.

Clients who have Afro hair like to try out smoother straight hairstyles, which they can do by adding extensions of European hair weft. Clients who have short fine flyaway hair like to have extensions to make their hair look longer and fuller.

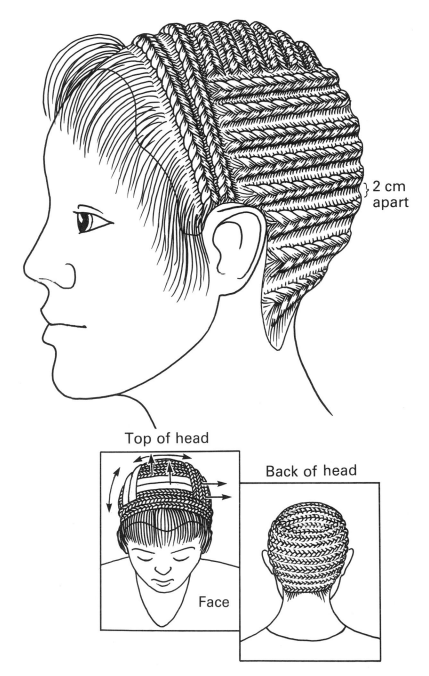

} 2 cm
apart

Top of head

Back of head

Face

Figure 6.16 *Cane rowing or corn rowing*

Preparation of client's head for weft extensions

Two methods are given here (see Figure 6.16).

Cane rowing

1 The short hair of the head is divided up into sections by thin partings.
2 The partings are positioned as required for the finished hairstyle.
3 The hair is taken at the beginning of a section and twisted between finger and thumb. The next piece of hair in the section is picked up with it, and the twisting carries on in this way to the end of the row. The twisted hair is kept very close to the scalp.
4 When the end of the row is reached, sew down securely with matching cotton.
5 Complete all sections in this manner.
6 If Afro hair, use hair oil when cane rowing.
7 If European hair, use a setting gel or wet the hair first.

Corn rowing

1 Prepare the head in the same way as for cane rowing, 1 and 2.
2 Take a small section of hair each time, divide into three small sections and plait them firmly so that they lie flat to the scalp.
3 Continue along section by picking up hair from the roots at short intervals and continuing the flat corn rowing.
4 When the end of the section is finished, twist ends to tidy, then neatly fold back and sew securely.

It must be explained here that, as with most hairstyles, one must adapt the client's hairline to give a natural look. Therefore the front hair may have to be left short in order to cover the sections made to sew the weft on. This will very much depend on how much hair the client has.

The number of sections needs to be worked out before the corn or cane rowing is started, because the amount of weaving required will have to be measured and woven to suit these measurements.

Prepare a weft by hand, weaving hair 30 cm long. Alternatively, if you are using synthetic fibre you can buy it already curled and machine wefted. You can also buy real human hair

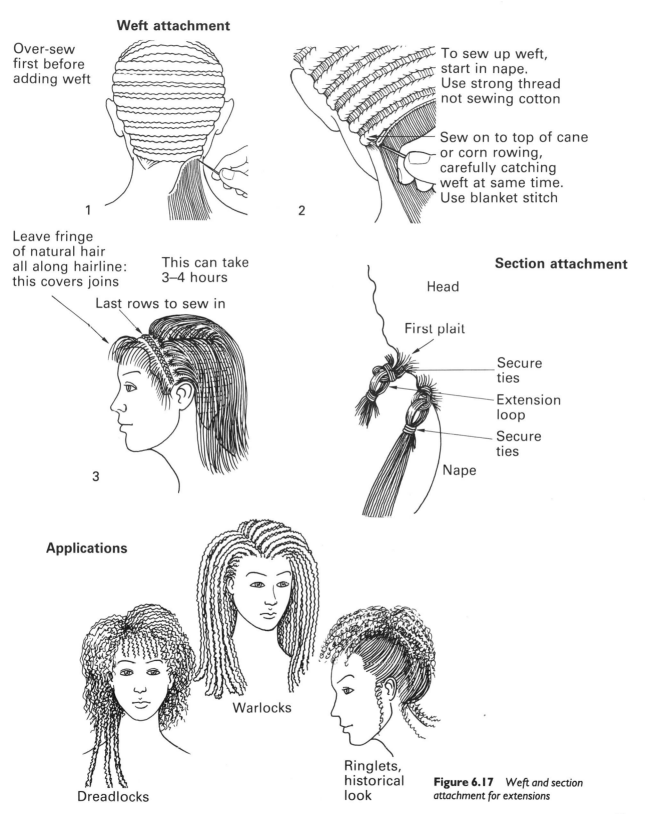

Weft attachment

Over-sew first before adding weft

To sew up weft, start in nape. Use strong thread not sewing cotton

Sew on to top of cane or corn rowing, carefully catching weft at same time. Use blanket stitch

1

2

Leave fringe of natural hair all along hairline: this covers joins

This can take 3–4 hours

Last rows to sew in

3

Section attachment

Head

First plait

Secure ties

Extension loop

Secure ties

Nape

Applications

Dreadlocks

Warlocks

Ringlets, historical look

Figure 6.17 *Weft and section attachment for extensions*

that has been reduced by acids and machine wefted; it will last four or five months.

Remember that if you make and sew the weft on carefully, you can use it many times.

Attachment of weft to the head

Start at the nape and sew each section carefully and securely to the cane or corn rowing (Figure 6.17). Continue working row by row up the head until you have completed all the sections.

Your client now looks as if she has a head of long European hair.

Dressing of the attached weft extensions

Real human hair weft

1 Trim to shape of hairstyle.
2 You can perm now if required.
3 You can set the hair with roller and clips.
4 You can blow dry into a style.
5 You can braid or use curling tongs.
6 You can dry under a hair dryer.
7 You can brush or comb into hairstyle.

Synthetic fibre weft

1 Trim to shape of hairstyle (do *not* use hair scissors).
2 The fibre is mainly permanently curled, so there is no requirement for extra hairdressing.
3 Does need care when sleeping because it can become tangled.
4 It is difficult to comb out quickly.

Maintenance of extensions

The use of a back wash is of great assistance.

Real human hair

1 Wash carefully with a mild shampoo. Do not rub the hair, just squeeze gently.
2 Rinse very well.
3 Use a good conditioner.
4 Do not rub to dry the hair. Just wrap a towel gently around the head to collect moisture.

5 Then comb out from the nape points to the roots, section by section until you complete the head.
6 Now carry on with normal hairdressing procedure for the style required.

Synthetic fibre

1 Wash carefully with shampoo in warm water. Do not rub the fibre, just squeeze gently.
2 Rinse well with cold water.
3 Place a large towel around the head to absorb moisture. Do not rub.
4 Let the fibre dry naturally before you comb it carefully section by section. Do *not* use heat to dry the fibre.
5 No hairdressing required.

The extensions will last a long time, but you must look after your client's hair by keeping it oiled. If any irritation occurs, remove the extensions carefully by unpicking the sewing and removing the weft. Unpick the corn or cane rowing carefully.

Section extensions (Figure 6.17)

I have shown you how to convert a whole head of short to medium hair using woven weft strips.

Equally, you can use extensions on a particular area of the head to create a specific hairstyle, e.g. pony tail, ringlets, dreadlocks, warlocks, long plaits. This time you use long sections of hair or synthetic fibre that has not been woven. These sections are attached individually to the area of the head required by the hairstyle.

Attachment of section of hair or fibre

This method requires two operators working together (Figure 6.17):

1 Take a small section of client's hair (4–5 cm long) and make a small tight plait. Tie and secure the ends.
2 Take a small section of the long false hair or fibre extensions and make a loop of hair at the root end. Tie and secure this loop.
3 Pass the little plait through the loop and tie and secure after looping the plait back on itself near the scalp.
4 For added strength you can wind the thread around both loops, then secure again. Use fine strong matching thread.

Style ideas

Figures 6.17, 6.18 and 6.19 illustrate various hairstyles:

1 The whole head can be carefully sectioned off and the hair or fibre attached in this manner. This creates a warlocks look.
2 The nape hair can be sectioned off and used to create a dreadlocks look.
3 The hair behind or in front of the ears can be sectioned off and hair or fibre added to create an historical hairstyle by adding ringlets or ragtails.
4 Brightly coloured hair extensions can be spaced over the head for a fun fantasy hairstyle.
5 Research into African hairstyles could help you create some ideas of your own – as well as improve your manual dexterity and patience.

White

Figure 6.18 *Style created using several different methods of false hair attachment*

Figure 6.19 *Style created using hair attachments at the crown area of the head*

7 Corrective make-up and hairstyling: fashion work

Corrective make-up

Study the face. Can it be improved for a particular purpose? If so, how?

A face has two sides. Which side to correct can be decided by covering first one side and then the other with a sheet of paper. Choose the better side.

If time and facilities allow, photograph the face and take normal and reverse prints. Cut both photographs down the middle. Switch the halves and stick them together. Now you have two photographs of the face with both sides matching. The less appealing face will show which side to correct.

Corrections are based on personal taste, which in turn is affected by current fashion. Fashion is usually concerned with individual features like eyebrows and lips. Colour is also dictated by fashion.

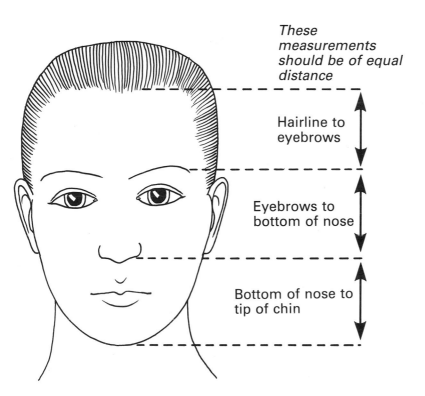

These measurements should be of equal distance

Hairline to eyebrows

Eyebrows to bottom of nose

Bottom of nose to tip of chin

Figure 7.1 *Classical proportions of the face for Europeans*

The classical proportions of the face are shown in Figure 7.1. Look at your model or yourself, and measure the actual proportions carefully. Write down how they differ from the classical proportions. The task of corrective make-up is to make actual proportions as close as possible to classical.

Two points to remember are:

1 If you want to make any part of the face smaller, you must make it darker.
2 If you want to emphasize any feature, you must make it lighter.

Below are instructions on applying these rules and minimizing any obvious irregularities. Some of the following corrections only work full face. Make work sheets of faces and practise using felt tips to fill in corrections (Figure 7.2: face patterns are given in Figures 3.2 and 3.3).

Base colour or foundation

1 Additional colour is needed for the foundation. Fashionable make-up colours may affect your choice.
2 If pale skin is the fashion, then lighten the foundation.
3 If summer tans are the fashion, then use a darker foundation.
4 The model's own colour will also affect colour selection. Choose a colour that looks attractive in the lighting or situation in which he/she will be seen.

Forehead

To lower a high forehead Take a basecolour three times darker than the foundation colour on the face. Darken the area next to the hairline and blend downwards very gradually so that it disappears into the foundation.

To raise a low forehead Take a base colour three times lighter than the foundation colour on the face. Lighten the area next to the hairline and blend downwards very gradually so that it disappears into the foundation. This attracts the eye upwards, emphasizing the height of the forehead.

To narrow a wide forehead Take a base colour three times darker than the foundation colour on the face. Shadow the temples and blend on to the front plane of the forehead. By decreasing

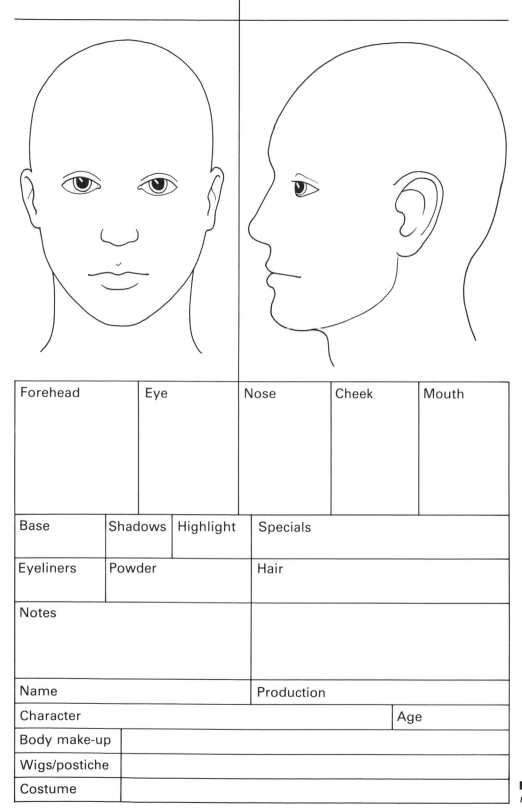

Forehead	Eye	Nose	Cheek	Mouth

Base	Shadows	Highlight	Specials	
Eyeliners	Powder		Hair	
Notes				
Name		Production		
Character			Age	
Body make-up				
Wigs/postiche				
Costume				

Figure 7.2 *Corrective make-up work sheet*

the actual width of the forehead, plane, this gives the illusion of the forehead turning sooner.

To widen a narrow forehead (sunken temples)   Take a base colour three times lighter than the base and highlight the temples. Blend into the hairline. This counteracts the natural shadows and gives the illusion of bringing them forward.

Noses

To make a nose look shorter   Apply deeper base colour under tip of nose and blend it up just over tip. Apply a short highlight on the upper part of the nose. This helps to draw the eye away from tip.

To make a nose look longer   Apply highlight down over tip of nose.

To widen a thin nose   Apply broad highlight down the centre of the nose. Blend carefully. This will broaden the front plane only. You could highlight the nostrils to attract eye outwards.

To thin a wide nose   Apply very thin highlight down the centre of the nose. Shadow the sides and nostrils. Blend the edges.

To slim a fat-ended nose   Apply wide shadow down the centre of the nose. Highlight the sides and nostrils. Blend the edges.

To slim a broad-ended nose   Shadow on each side of the nose.

To straighten a crooked nose   Apply narrow highlight down the top of the nose. Apply shadow on either side and wherever there is a natural highlight that shows the crookedness.

If you wanted to change the profile of a nose you would have to use three dimensional additions, for example, putty or a false nose.

Face shapes

Shape shadows

Shape shadows are used to soften the features that you do not like. Figure 7.3 shows some examples.

Square face Take a large brush from the jawline up to the cheek-bone. If there is a large forehead, narrow it now.

Long face and oval face Take a large brush. Start near the jaw-bone and take it up to the temple area. If there is a high forehead, use shadow at this point.

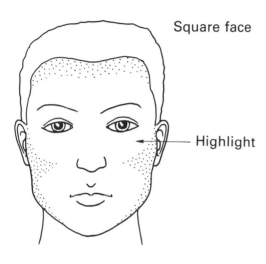

Square face

— Highlight

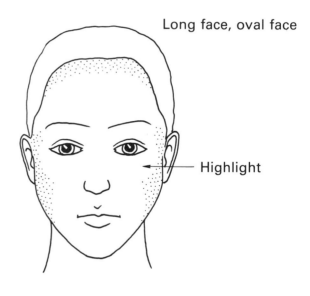

Long face, oval face

— Highlight

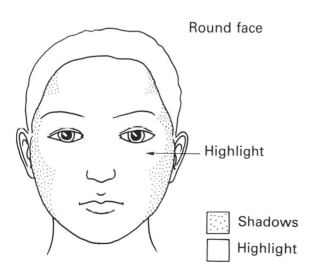

Round face

— Highlight

::: Shadows

☐ Highlight

Figure 7.3 *Using shape shadows*

Round face   Take a large brush. Start at the jawline and fade it as you reach the temples. If there is a high forehead, use shadow on the sides to help reduce roundness.

Shape highlights

Use foundation two shades lighter than the base. These highlights are used to accentuate the features that you like.

Square face   Highlight the cheek-bones to give extra width.

Long face and oval face   Highlight the cheek-bones to give extra width.

Round face   Keep highlighted area more in the centre of the cheek-bone area.

Jawline and chin

To lessen a square or prominent chin   Shadow the part that needs rounding off or toning down. Carry the shadow both under and over the jaw-bone. Blend it into the foundation.

To make a chin firm and youthful   Apply stripe of highlight all along jaw-bone, softening the lower edge and blending in top edge to foundation. A stripe of shadow can be run along under the bone and both edges blended.

Chin juts out   Darken the whole chin with a light shadow.

Very long chin   Shorten by shadowing the lower part and blend in.

Very short chin   Highlight the lower part.

Chin too square   Round off corners with shadows.

Chin too pointed   Flatten the point with square shadow.

Double chin   Minimize by shadowing it, making it less noticeable.

Face lifts

These are used only for theatrical make-ups.
   Plaster with cord is stuck on to the jawline and on both sides of the neck. The cords are tied on the top of the head and covered with a wig. In this way the face skin is pulled tight.

Eyes

Corrective make-up for eyes is shown in Figure 7.4. Eyes should be width of an eye apart.

Lips

Wide lips   Cover edge of lips with foundation. Use a lip brush to draw an outline that ends before it reaches the corners of the mouth. Fill in the outline with lipstick.

Thin lips   Cover edge of lips with foundation. Using a lip brush, with a steady hand outline above the natural lips with pale lipstick. Then fill in with a slightly darker lipstick. Do not use dark lipsticks as this would emphasize the thin lips.

Full lips   If the lips require slimming down, outline with a deep lip colour just inside the true lip line. Fill in with lipstick of medium colour.

Out of proportion lips (mismatched)   Where the top lip is slim and the bottom lip is fat, or vice versa, use the above techniques for each lip.

Uneven lips   Decide which side is best, then even the other side to match. Draw an even outline and then fill in.

Always blot lipstick with tissue each time you apply it. This makes it last longer.

Cosmetic camouflage: application sequence

1 *Prepare skin thoroughly*   Use a good cleanser or soap and water. Remove gently with cotton wool or tissue.
2 *Tone skin after cleansing*   This step is important because if there is any remaining oiliness on the skin it would make the camouflage cream 'slip'. Witch hazel may be used for toning.
3 *Moisturizing*   This is only necessary if skin is excessively dry. Use a light water based moisturizer, e.g. Oil of Ulay.
4 *Apply camouflage cream*   Apply cream thinly, with fingertips or brush, depending on technique that is used. The blemish should be thoroughly covered with the cream extending an inch beyond the blemish. Apply camouflage cream layer by layer until the blemish is completely concealed and blend the edges into the clear skin.
5 *Shading* Use shading cream to restore the natural shadows under and over the eyes, along the side and

1 *Eyes set wide apart*
Shade eye area and pencil in eyebrow to make eyes appear closer to nose

2 *Eyes set close together*
Shade eye area and pencil in eyebrow to make eyes appear farther from nose

False eyelashes can help

3 *Shading to turn eyes up* at outer corners
Emphasized by lining
Should not surround eye

4 *Shading to droop eye* at outer corners

5 *To make eye smaller*
Highlight around the eye only

6 *To make eye larger*

Eye shadow colour depends on:
Colour eyes
personal preference
costume colour
fashion
male: brown, grey

Mascara eyelashes:
Always apply after powder

Figure 7.4 *Corrective make-up for eyes*

under the nose and on the chin. Use also to darken your shade of camouflage cream as the skin tans. This step is only necessary if the blemish is extensive, or covers one of the above mentioned areas.

6 *Cream rouge* Use cream rouge to restore the natural colour of the cheeks if necessary.

7 *Grey toner* On men use grey toner to restore the greyish tone of the beard when blemish is in this area.

8 *Finishing powder* Dry and set cover cream with colourless finishing powder. Apply generously by 'fluffing' on with cotton wool. Press in gently using a rocking motion but do not rub. Leave powder for approximately ten minutes to set, then remove excess with large 'fluff' brush.

9 *Finish* To achieve a natural effect dab off any excess powder with a lightly damp sponge or tissue.

10 *Client advice* Most good cosmetic camouflage creams, e.g. Veil, Covermark, are waterproof. Therefore the client may swim when wearing this cream. However, the area should not be rubbed dry but patted.

For facial blemishes after the procedure for covering has been followed including powdering, a water-based make-up may be applied on top.

Camouflage

There is a special range of make-up for covering birthmarks and any form of skin discoloration. You need to follow the manufacturer's instructions for use, and you need a very good eye for colour. The product is called Covermark and is available from Medexport Ltd, Arundel, West Sussex, England.

Mixing

Skin varies in colour from one part of the body to another. People's complexions can be broadly identified as pale, medium and dark skinned. However, we know that this breaks down into many combinations. If you study the range of colour on just one face you can understand the complexities of a portrait painter's palette.

Someone who is good at camouflage has a portrait painter's skills in using the special make-up, which has true cover-all qualities. A birthmark can be covered so that the area blended invisibly joins the rest of the skin area.

If you have a good eye for colour mixing then, with practice, you should be able to use camouflage make-up well. Practice for this kind of mixing comes when you block out eyebrows. You need to make up the area so that it matches exactly the skin around the eyebrow.

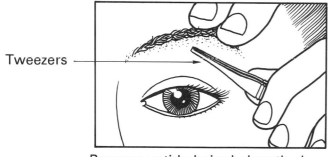

Remove untidy hairs below the brow

Examples of eyebrow shapes

 Thin

 Thick

 Normal

 Straight

 Arched

Figure 7.5 *Plucking and shaping eyebrows*

Eyebrow shaping

Eyebrows help to define and frame the face. Well-shaped eyebrows help to give an appearance of good grooming. Their shaping is partly governed by the general shape of the face and by the dictates of fashion.

To shape eyebrows, one must work under a good light and use a pair of tweezers. They can be automatic or plain, either straight edged or rounded.

Method

Consult a client as to her wishes. You can always remove further hairs if requested, but you cannot replace them if you have removed too many.

1 Remove all the make-up on and under the brows.
2 Wipe the tweezers with spirit or antiseptic.
3 Wipe the brow with cotton wool and antiseptic lotion. Wipe frequently during the procedure to remove stray hairs and to cool the brow.
4 Gently stretch the skin between two fingers, pressing on the skin behind the hair, and pluck in the direction of hair growth.

Hair should mainly be removed from behind the brow. Stray hair between the brows and at the temples can also be removed.

- Strong, long or discoloured hairs in the brow may be removed if they do not alter the brow line.
- Overplucked or shaved eyebrows should be left and lightly trimmed regularly until a good shape is achieved.
- Heavy brows should not be plucked to a fine line in one session – the client should get used to a gradual shaping. It could also be rather painful.

Some clients find it more painful than others. For these clients prepare cotton wool patters and place in a fridge. When you have finished the shaping place these over the brow to cool the skin. See Figure 7.5 for examples of eyebrow shapes.

Spots

For health reasons, these should be left untouched by make-up. However, they may need to be covered for a particular make-up.

First treat the spot with a little diluted antiseptic to make sure that it is clean. Choose a flesh-coloured spot cream and dab it on the spot using a special brush. Then apply foundation with care.

Frown lines, crow's feet and smile lines

1 Apply base foundation.
2 Take a very fine brush (size 2).
3 Use pale-coloured erasing cream or greasepaint make-up.
4 Paint the cream along the frown lines, keeping the line very fine.
5 Blend it in using your finger tips, touching lightly and evenly as you work along the lines.
6 Powder to fix make-up.

Dark shadows

These may occur under the eyes and elsewhere.

1 Use the same technique as for frown lines.
2 Apply base foundation over the face and neck.
3 Use brush or finger tips to cover the dark area with pale-coloured erasing cream or greasepaint make-up.
4 Blend the pale make-up outwards with little tapping movements of the finger tips. Be careful not to drag the skin.
5 Powder to fix make-up.

High colouring, broken veins

Apply green foundation cream with a sponge very thinly over the offending area; the green cancels the pink in the skin. Apply base foundation over the green foundation and powder to set.

Corrective hairstyles

Styling the hair with facial features in mind is as important as using corrective make-up for the face (Figure 7.6).

Wigs and hair pieces can be used to create illusion for character work, but can also be used for fashion purposes if the model's hair is not suitable for the desired hairstyle. Most actors and actresses like to use their own hair whenever possible.

Figure 7.6 *Corrective hairstyles*

Oval face   If you have an oval face, any style will suit you. Look at Figure 7.6 for other face shapes.

Square face   Avoid severe styles as they make the jawline more obvious. Choose a soft full curly style. Take the squareness away by making each side of the face different, e.g. side parting, full fringe or one side tucked behind one ear.

Long thin face   Avoid the severe long straight look. Shorten the long face with a full fringe. Add width to the face by cutting off length and introducing a soft bouncy movement to the lower part of the face.

Round face   Avoid full round styles which only give extra width to the face. Take away roundness by adding height to make the face look longer. Make the sides different with an off-centre fringe.

The length of the neck should also be considered when making the final choice of hairstyle.

Assessments

1 Make your forehead (a) wider (b) narrower (c) higher (d) lower.
2 Using only greasepaint, change the shape of your nose, making it (a) longer and narrower (b) shorter (c) broader (d) flatter.
3 Make your eyes (a) farther apart (b) closer together. Make one eye (c) smaller (d) larger.
4 Change the shape of your eyebrows without blocking them out.
5 Study your own face. Note prominent bones; size of eyes, nose, mouth and chin; height of forehead; shape and thickness of eyebrows; shape, width and fullness of lips. Decide which features you would like to change for your corrective make-up. Write them down, filling in a work sheet. Do a complete corrective make-up on yourself. Take photographs before and after your work.

Make-up for fashion work

The creation of glamorous photographic make-up for colour film will illustrate many of the techniques of corrective make-up, and is an essential project in its own right.

Equipment

Complete make-up box.
Make-up brushes, stipple sponges etc.
Bowl of prepared damp patters.
Gown and protective clothing for model.
Powder.
Black eyebrow pencil or eyeliner.
False eyelashes (single ones are best).
Graphite pencil.
Base foundation: select colour as close as possible to the client's own skin tone.
Highlights: choose a foundation two shades lighter than foundation colour.
Shadows: choose a foundation two shades darker than foundation colour.

Preparation

Prepare the model. Cleanse the face.
Take a photograph before you begin your work. Note any corrective make-up you may need to do, using a work sheet such as that in Figure 7.7.

Method

1 Apply black eyebrown pencil to top eyeline. Extend beyond outer corners. Blend this down into the eyelashes.
2 Apply a thin layer of eye shadow along the lash line and blend this softly up towards brow.
3 Apply dark shadow foundation under chin and along jawline, and blend down into top of the neck.
4 Apply some dark shadow foundation under cheek-bone. Push brush under cheek-bone and blend upwards, avoiding top of cheek-bone (Figure 7.8).

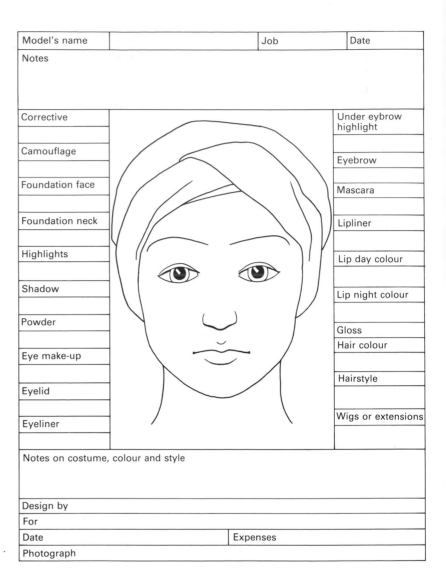

Model's name		Job	Date

Notes

Corrective		Under eybrow highlight
Camouflage		Eyebrow
Foundation face		Mascara
Foundation neck		Lipliner
Highlights		Lip day colour
Shadow		Lip night colour
Powder		Gloss
Eye make-up		Hair colour
Eyelid		Hairstyle
Eyeliner		Wigs or extensions

Notes on costume, colour and style

Design by	
For	
Date	Expenses
Photograph	

Figure 7.7 *Photographic make-up work sheet*

5 Now take base foundation colour on to a sponge and stipple thinly and evenly over the complete face, i.e. over all previous make-up.

6 Apply a little highlight under the eyes. Blend into base colour towards cheeks (see figure).

7 Apply a little highlight on each cheek-bone and blend slightly (see figure).

8 Take shadow colour and shade along top jaw and blend up towards cheek. Remember you are trying to make the jawline oval in shape (see figure).

9 Set the make-up well with colourless powder.

10 Take a damp patter to remove excess powder.

11 If more eye shadow is required, add it at this point.

12 Repaint eyeline using fine brush.

13 Using same brush, paint line under eyes at the outer edge of lashes only.

14 Sketch in eyebrows with graphite pencil. Use short strokes. Brush and comb only if the eyebrows are strong.

15 Add blusher for shape and colour to the cheeks, chin, nose and forehead.

16 Add lip colour with brush to mouth shape. Add lip gloss.

17 Apply mascara to lashes, holding damp cotton wool pad underneath to protect skin.

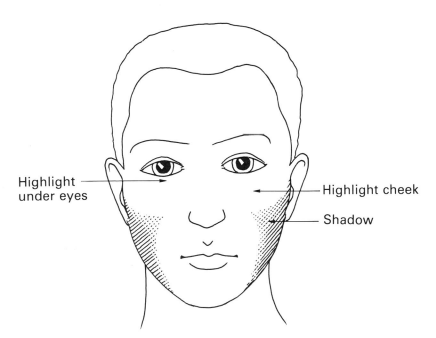

Highlight under eyes

Highlight cheek

Shadow

Figure 7.8 *Shading jaw and under cheek*

18 Add false eyelashes if required (see notes on application, page 105).

19 Dress hair to complete the make-up, or add a wig: see next section.

20 Check neck, hairline and ears carefully.

21 Place model under very strong light to see if make-up works. Take notes if you need to make anything stronger or softer.

22 Take a photograph under strong light.
23 Take another photograph in daylight. If possible, take black and white as well as colour photographs to compare.

False eyelashes

There are two main types of false eyelashes:

1 Individual lashes.
2 Strip lashes.

Individual lashes

Individual lashes can be used in addition to natural lashes. Each lash consists of several fine hairs in a tiny root (bulb). The root is attached with adhesive to the base of the existing natural lash, not the eyelid. The result is a natural look.

Points to remember

1 Lashes are waterproof.
2 Will last as long as natural lash to which they are attached.

Strip lashes

Strip lashes are produced as a set, to be secured along the edge of the eyelid with adhesive. They are available in varying thicknesses, the finest being for daytime use.

Points to remember

1 Trim lashes to correct size before application. Trim end where lashes are longest – this will be the outside. Measure model's width of eye first and then cut lashes as required. Cutting is nearly always required. Remember natural lashes will vary in length depending on stage of hair growth. Always cut *into* lashes, not *across*, for more than natural length with sharp, short scissors.
2 Never apply lashes to inner corner of eye but approximately 5 mm away from it.
3 Special adhesive may be required if the client is allergic to the normal one.

4 Remove by holding outside and gently peeling off towards nose so as not to drag lid.

Application for individual lashes

1 Apply make-up, up to foundation and powder.
2 Pour a few drops of eyelash adhesive onto a piece of foil.
3 Take tweezers and hold individual lash. Dip knotted end into adhesive (a very small amount). Start your application on the outer edge of the eyes.
4 Place lash on top of the natural lash with the knotted end as close to, but not touching, the eyelid.
5 Support the lash for a few seconds while adhesive works.
6 You can apply up to about fifteen lashes per eye.
7 If necessary, use a curling appliance. Trim the lashes.
8 You can use an eye liner but try not to use mascara as this cannot easily be removed without removing the false lashes.

Application for strip lashes

1 Clean eyelid and ensure free of dirt and grease.
2 Apply adhesive along straight edge of false lashes using orange wood stick (pointed end) and glue off palette.
3 Using blunt end of orange wood stick press centre of lashes onto eyelid as close to natural lash as possible. Press the lashes down working along the lid first one way and then the other.
4 Remove any excess adhesive immediately as once dried it is difficult to see to remove. If left on the skin it will feel tacky and uncomfortable.
5 Blend together false lashes and natural lashes with a mascara brush.
6 Using eyeliner fill in any gaps on edge of the lids.
7 Apply mascara only if absolutely necessary and first from top and then from underneath.

False lashes are rarely applied to bottom lashes as they can look heavy. Strip lashes can be reused time and time again. Always remove old adhesive with soapy water.

Curling false eyelashes to create natural look

1 Wash lashes if necessary.
2 Tissue paper and round pencil are needed.

3 Lay lashes, right way up, onto tissue at one end of tissue length.
4 Place pencil on top of lashes.
5 Roll tissue tightly, starting at pencil end using palms of hands and fingers.
6 Put elastic band around each end.
7 Leave for several hours or overnight.
8 Lashes ready.

Postiche and wigs for fashion work

When you have completed a photographic glamour make-up, it can be useful to have a selection of various modern hairstyles to try on the model.

If the model already has plenty of beautiful hair, you probably will not require a wig. However, if the hair requires washing or dressing and you do not have a great deal of time, this is the opportunity to use a wig. If the model's hairline causes a problem, just comb out the model's own hair and show the natural hairline by combing the model's hair back into the wig hair.

Various styles and colours of wigs offer a wide range of choice.

There are other possible fashion reasons for using wigs:

1 The model has short hair, whereas long hair would look better.
2 The model has long hair, whereas a short style is required by the photographer.
3 The model's hair is fine and flyaway, and it is a wet and windy day. A wig would stand up to these conditions.
4 You are working on location and it is not possible to carry out hairdressing.

Preparing the head for a wig

Equipment

Tape measure.
Gown.
Dressing comb.
Tail comb or spatula.
Box of hair grips.
Box of hair pins.
Fine hair net.
Elastic bands.

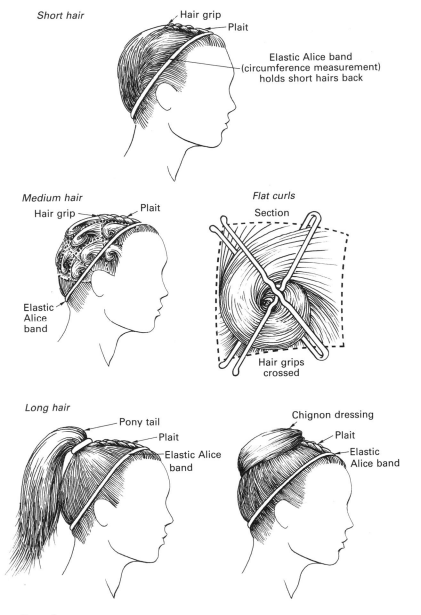

Figure 7.9 *Preparing head hair for wig wear*

Procedure

First measure the model's head circumference. This is the area to be covered by the elastic Alice band (Figure 7.9). Now measure the wig circumference by turning the wig inside-out. If the measurements are compatible, make the Alice band using thin elastic. Remember to allow for the model's own hair when taken up under the wig.

Sew a postiche comb into the wig. This is a small comb which is sewn just back from the centre front of the wig. It holds the wig firm and stops it sliding back when dressing it (Figure 7.10). This is not needed if the model has no hair.

If model has short hair

1 Take a section of the model's own hair out in the centre front hairline. Make this into a small tight plait. Secure the end with a hair grip (Figure 7.9).
2 Put elastic Alice band over the head to the neck.
3 Comb the rest of the hair back from the face.
4 Now bring the elastic Alice band up and around the head to hold the hair back.

If model has medium hair

1 Take hair from the centre front hairline and make a small plait (Figure 7.9).
2 Divide the hair up into small equal sections all over the head.
3 Pin curl each section flat to the head. Use hairgrips crossed to hold the curl.
4 Place elastic Alice band around the head and over some of the sections.
5 Decide if you require a hair net.

If model has long hair

1 Take hair from the centre front hairline and make a small plait (Figure 7.9).
2 Make a pony tail, holding the hair tightly with an elastic band.
3 Now make a flat chignon top knot of the long hair. Fix securely with hair grips and hair pins.
4 Place hair net over the chignon.
5 Use the elastic Alice band to keep short hair tidy.

How to place wig on head

1 Take a wig and turn it inside-out. Look and find the centre front positional spring with the postiche comb.
2 Place this centre of the wig on to the centre of the hairline. Push the postiche comb into the front of the model's front hairline plait (Figure 7.10).
3 Now ease the wig down to both sides by the ears.
4 Then ease the wig over the crown and pull down into the nape.
5 Check ear positional springs are level from side to side. In other words, check the wig is on the head straight.

6 Take a tail comb or spatula and check the model's hairline, tidying stray hairs that may have come out from under the wig. Push this hair back under carefully.
7 The wig is now ready to comb out.

The wig is kept in position by a tension spring or an elastic in the nape. Positional springs are sewn into the wig to keep its shape. Some wigs have drawn elastics that have to be tied when the wig is in position.

How to remove wig from head

1 Take the back nape of the wig with both hands, and lift it up and forward.
2 Place it on a malleable block of the correct size.

How to place hair-lace front wig on head

For theatre, television and film:

1 Prepare model's head, making sure that the hairline is very smooth. Do not make a plait this time.
2 Place the wig on the head in the normal way. This wig may have a blender, which is an extra piece of material that goes under the hair-lace hairline, but is shorter than the hair-lace. Be sure it covers the model's natural hairline. The hair-lace front wig must be placed on the head before make-up has been applied.
3 The hair-lace must be carefully stuck down using spirit gum. Apply spirit gum along the hairline under the lace and down to the temples and ears on both sides.
4 Let the spirit gum go tacky.
5 Now carefully press down the hair-lace with a damp sponge.
6 When well dry you can apply make-up over the hair-lace.

How to remove hair-lace front wig from head

1 Take a medium flat brush.
2 Take some spirit gum remover on to the brush.
3 Protect eyes with a towel.
4 Now brush gently on to gummed areas of hairline.
5 When it has soaked for a while, lift up the edges carefully with the brush.
6 When the hairline has lifted without force, lift the nape of the wig at the back and pull up and forward. The hair-lace comes off last.

7 Surgical spirit can also be used to remove spirit gum.

8 The hair-lace must be cleaned carefully with acetone after each use, even if the wig is not. This will remove spirit gum and make-up.

9 Place on to a malleable block until ready to wear again.

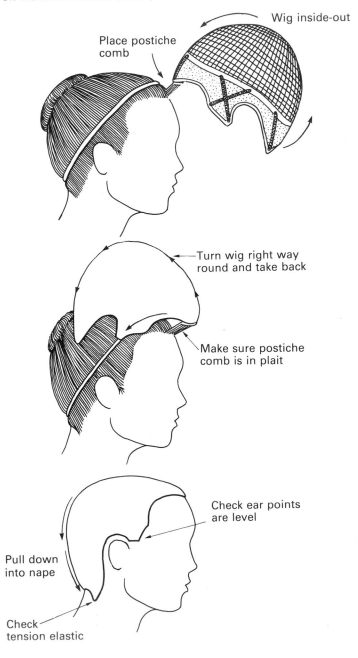

Sit model in front of mirror, stand behind model

Wig inside-out

Place postiche comb

Turn wig right way round and take back

Make sure postiche comb is in plait

Check ear points are level

Pull down into nape

Check tension elastic

Figure 7.10 *Placing a wig*

8 Wig types and applications

Wigs are used:

- to change the character
- to change the sex
- to create an historical hairstyle
- to achieve baldness (bald wigs)
- to make you look older or younger
- to create a fantasy or an illusion
- to make you glamorous
- to signify an office (legal wigs) or a religious occasion.

Identification of wigs

To identify a wig type you must first look at the way the wig has been constructed. This will tell you if it has:

- a hand-made foundation
- a machine-made foundation
- hand-knotted hair
- machine-made weft
- hand-made weft
- a combination of machine weft and hand-knotted drawn-through parting work.

In general, if a wig has any hand work then it is more valuable than one without. If the foundation is hand made, the hair knotted into it is likely to be human hair.

If the foundation is a frame of elastic strips or a closed elastic net, and a machine weft is sewn on to the foundation, then the weft is made of synthetic fibre or of hair reduced by acids for European use. Hair that is reduced by acids has had its outer cuticle removed. This means that:

1 It cannot tangle up.
2 It can be used in a weft-making machine.
3 It can be washed in shampoo and water without tangling up.
4 It is weaker in structure than a human hair.

Cleaning and dressing wigs

The main reason for identifying wig types is to be able to clean them without damaging them. There are two choices:

1 To wash them using shampoo and water.
2 To dry clean them using industrial spirit.

Sometimes manufacturers help by placing labels inside the wigs, but this is not always the case.

When you have decided whether a wig is made of real hair, synthetic fibre or reduced hair, it can be cleaned as follows:

1 Real knotted hair needs dry cleaning.
2 Real wefted hair needs dry cleaning.
3 Machine wefted hair needs a shampoo wash.
4 Machine wefted fibre needs a shampoo wash.
5 A combination wig, i.e. machine wefted hair/fibre plus knotted drawn-through parting work, needs a shampoo wash.

The wig type also determines the possibilities for dressing, as follows.

Dry cleaned wigs/postiche

Because such wigs are made of real hair, we have a wide range of possibilities.

The wig, after dry cleaning, must be blocked up on to the correct size of malleable block for that wig. The malleable block should be protected by polythene if any colouring or chemicals are to be used.

When the wig is blocked up correctly, it can be wetted with water for setting, cutting and blow drying. It can also be carefully permed, dyed or bleached. This is advanced wig and hairdressing work.

The wig is then slowly dried in a postiche oven, under a hood hair dryer or in an airing cupboard.

Shampoo washed wigs/postiche

These wigs, after shampooing and rinsing, must be shaken to remove excess water, then placed on a towel. They can be hung up to dry or put on a block to dry naturally.

They have their own made-in hairstyle. It is best not to comb them until they are dry. You could trim them a little to change the style, but that is all. You must not use heat on these wigs.

Chapter 10 discusses the cleaning and dressing of wigs in more detail.

Types of wig

Weft wigs

Simple weft wig

This is a mass-produced cheap wig in various sizes. The foundation is made of machine-sewn vegetable net. The machine weft is made from synthetic fibre or reduced hair, and is machine sewn on to the foundation.

If the wig is made of synthetic fibre, it cannot have its style changed. If it is made of hair reduced by acids, it can be styled with limitations. It is used on stage or screen, and is ideal for crowd scenes.

Stretch weft wig

This is a mass-produced cheap wig made to fit most people. Its foundation is made of machine-sewn elastic net. The machine weft is made from synthetic fibre or reduced hair, and the weft is machine sewn on to the foundation.

It is washed and used in the same way as a simple weft wig. Once the elasticity has gone, the wig is finished.

Fashion weft stretch wigs

These wigs are mass produced for the fashion trade. They are made to fit most people. The price range is medium to expensive, and the wigs are made in a wide range of modern hairstyles and colours.

The foundation is made of elastic strips forming an open skeletal base. The strips enable the wearer to stay cool, but if the wind lifts the hair you can see what is underneath. The machine-made weft is machine sewn in layers attached to the skeletal base (Figure 8.1). The weft can be made of synthetic fibre or hair reduced by acids.

The top of the wig has a large area of hand-knotted drawn-through parting style work. This is very effective, as it looks as if the hair is growing from the scalp. We call this a combination wig (Figure 8.2).

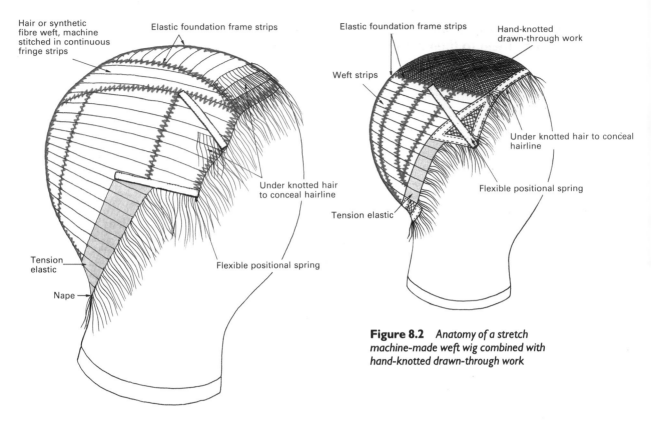

Hair or synthetic fibre weft, machine stitched in continuous fringe strips

Elastic foundation frame strips

Under knotted hair to conceal hairline

Flexible positional spring

Tension elastic

Nape

Figure 8.1 *Anatomy of a stretch machine-made weft wig*

Elastic foundation frame strips

Weft strips

Hand-knotted drawn-through work

Under knotted hair to conceal hairline

Flexible positional spring

Tension elastic

Figure 8.2 *Anatomy of a stretch machine-made weft wig combined with hand-knotted drawn-through work*

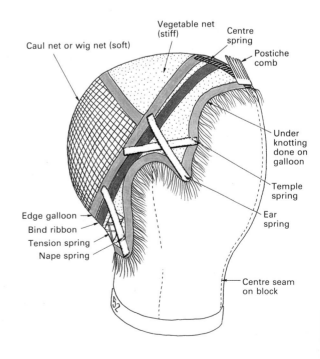

Vegetable net (stiff)

Centre spring

Postiche comb

Caul net or wig net (soft)

Under knotting done on galloon

Temple spring

Ear spring

Edge galloon

Bind ribbon

Tension spring

Nape spring

Centre seam on block

Figure 8.3 *Anatomy of a hand-made wig*

After washing, these wigs only require shaking, brushing or combing to return them to their set style. You cannot change this style.

These wigs are very cheap, easy to look after and easy to wear if you have hair of your own. If the synthetic fibre in the wig is the new type of matt finish, then it can be used for television and stage. (Synthetic fibre used to have an unnatural shine which made it unsuitable for television and film use.)

There are a number of disadvantages to these wigs:

1 They are light in weight but not to wear.
2 They fade easily in strong light.
3 Their life tends to be short in comparison with hand-made knotted real hair wigs.
4 With constant use, the set style can fall out and you cannot reset it successfully.
5 The elastic foundation perishes so that it no longer fits the head.
6 The fibre becomes dead looking and the ends of the fibres often split.

Knotted wigs

Hand-made foundation and hand-knotted real human hair

This wig is usually made to measure, and hence the price range is medium to very expensive. It will, of course, be an excellent fit. There is a choice of weight, and a choice of hair colour, length and quality. National Health wigs are of this type at the moment.

The foundation is made of hand-sewn or machine-sewn vegetable nets, both using a galloon base. The hair is always hand knotted to the foundation (Figure 8.3). The life of this wig is usually about seven years; the foundation wears out before the hair.

These wigs should be dry cleaned. They need regular setting and dressing by a wig hairdresser. Thus care is expensive. NHS clients are subsidized.

You can have a variety of hairstyles. The colour can be changed, and the wig can be permed or bleached.

This wig is the best type for a bald person. It is good value for private use and for theatrical, television and film work, and has a long life if looked after.

Figure 8.4 *Knotted wig with hair-lace front*

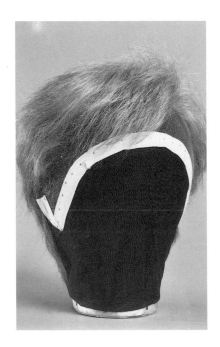

Figure 8.5 *Knotted wig with hair-lace front*

Knotted wig with hair-lace front

This is a theatrical wig (Figure 8.4). It differs from the previous wig in that it has a very fine see-through net, which we call hair-lace. This net is sewn across the front hairline of the wig, coming down on to the forehead. This enables us to knot an actual hairline for theatrical and media use. The net can be covered with make-up and become invisible.

Styling and dressing procedures are similar to those for the previous wig. However, note that this wig needs special attention when it is blocked up on a malleable block. The hair-lace front must be protected from tearing (Figure 8.5). The front must also be protected from discoloration.

The hair-lace front can be changed if it becomes damaged or if a different hairline is required. This wig is expensive but can have a long adaptable life on stage or screen. Theatrical wigmakers mostly make this type of wig for sale or hire.

Theatrical wig made of all fine hair-lace net

This wig can be made to measure (Figures 8.6 and 8.7). The front hairline is knotted to shape, and the hairstyle can be short or long. It can be made fairly quickly as it has no galloon sewing. The price range is medium to expensive.

The foundation is made of several pieces of very fine nets, sewn and moulded on to the correct size of wooden block. The wig is then knotted all over. Theatre companies with workshops mostly produce this type of wig. They can be easily remodelled and reused.

The wig should be dry cleaned if real hair is used. It needs good blocking up before being wetted, especially with the hair-lace hairline front. These wigs are more delicate than the previous two types, so they require more care when setting and dressing. Otherwise you can treat them the same as for the hair-lace front wig.

These wigs are used for stage and screen. They are very light and cool to wear, and very natural looking. They are not usually on offer to or required by the general public. However, some people who are bald and elderly do like to have lightweight wigs of this type instead of the heavy foundations found on the NHS wigs.

Wig applications

Stage, television and film

The principal actors and actresses usually have hand-made real hair wigs made for them. These wigs then fit beautifully. The hair is a good quality. When a production is finished, wigs can be stored for reuse and altered to fit other actors and actresses for new productions.

In amateur stage productions, the principal actors and actresses can hire quality wigs from theatrical wigmakers. Wigs of the right size, colour and hairstyle are sent to the company. The wardrobe mistress usually keeps an assortment of wigs, including some ready-made weft types, which would be used for all manner of productions.

For film and television, crowd scenes usually require a great many wigs. These can be mass-produced weft wigs or knotted wigs of various kinds. Usually real hair is preferred.

Some wigs for the stage, such as pantomime wigs, can be made of white nylon. Nylon is not usually used for film and television because of the unnatural shine. However, the everyday type of wig works well on the stage, particularly if it is made of matt finish nylon fibre.

Figure 8.6 *Hand-made theatrical wig*

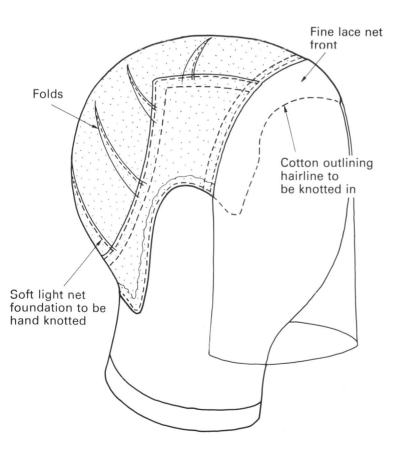

Fine lace net front

Folds

Cotton outlining hairline to be knotted in

Soft light net foundation to be hand knotted

Figure 8.7 *Anatomy of a hand-made theatrical wig*

Individual use for fashion

Hand-made wigs

Individual clients can buy hand-made wigs using real human hair, custom made or off the peg. The price will range from medium to expensive, depending mostly on the colour and quality of the hair. These wigs look and wear very well. Some people use their own hairlines.

Regular cleaning and dressing will be expensive. It is difficult to find hairdressers that are skilled at looking after these wigs; they are usually sent back to the makers for redressing. If maintained correctly, these wigs will last a long time.

Store weft wigs (Figures 8.1 and 8.2)

These are mass produced in various colours and styles. Some are better made than others, and usually the price reflects the value. The good weft wigs tend to be a little cheaper than hand-knotted wigs.

The better weft wigs do in fact have hand knotting over the centre front and crown areas. This knotting is of the drawn-through parting variety. It looks very natural, as if the hair is growing from the scalp.

Because these wigs are made to a specific style, they are easy to look after. They only require you to follow the manufacturer's directions, which are usually to wash, rinse, shake and dry naturally. These wigs do not like heat, for example from the sun, hair dryers, ovens and heated rollers.

If human hair is used, it will not be good quality. If synthetic fibre is used, the new matt finish fibre is the best. These wigs look and wear very well but only last in good condition for a short time by comparison with a custom-made wig. They are hot to wear, as the materials are all synthetic.

Wigs for health reasons (Figure 8.3)

Hand-made knotted real hair wigs (National Health wigs)

You are allowed two wigs at the beginning of your baldness, and then a new wig every seven years. You are only allowed National Health wigs if there is proof that your hair will not grow again.

These wigs are preferred by people who are bald. They are cooler to wear than a weft wig. They feel more secure, because if the wind blows the wig will not show baldness underneath. They are made to measure.

These wigs do have to be properly maintained by a skilled wigdresser. This can be expensive. However, some help with cleaning and dressing costs is given by the NHS. If properly managed, they wear well and look natural.

Store weft wigs (Figures 8.1 and 8.2)

These wigs are medium to expensive, as already stated.

They are easy to put on and maintain, and because of this they are popular with people who are in hospital for various reasons, for example if they are unable to use their arms, or if they have lost some part of the hair on their head, either temporarily or permanently. Simply knowing that their greasy or untidy hair is tucked under a wig during visiting times can be a great morale booster. Friends and nurses can easily put the wigs on for patients.

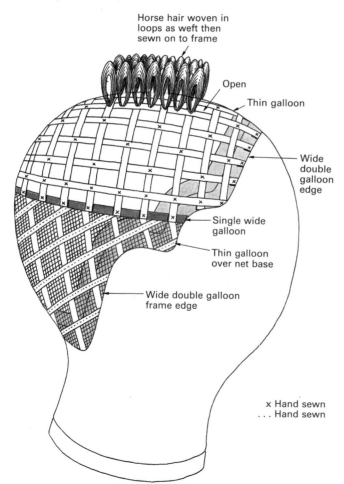

Figure 8.8 *Anatomy of a legal wig*

Elderly people who can no longer reach to comb their hair find these a great comfort. They keep the head warm and are more attractive than some types of head wear.

There is a good range in grey, white and 'salt and pepper' wigs.

Fun and party wigs

A wide variety of fun wigs is available. They have become very popular with the younger generation.

They are usually made of synthetic weft and fibre, in very bright colours and outrageous styles. They range widely in price; the clown type can be very cheap.

Legal wigs

The legal wig is still necessary in England (Figure 8.8). They are made by a specialist firm in London, using hair from horses' manes. They can be ordered or made to measure.

Large full-bottomed wigs are worn by judges, mainly for state occasions.

Hair loss

There are a variety of causes and types of hair loss:

- disease of the scalp
- constitutional disorders
- unknown cause in youth
- old age (senile baldness)
- loss in patches
- baldness of mother after giving birth
- use of drugs
- hair breakage (bad hair dressing can be the cause).

Baldness or alopecia means the loss of hair, whether on the scalp, in other places or over the whole body. It is a condition largely confined to industrialized peoples; it is rarely found in indigenous peoples who live an open air life.

Hair attachment

There are six forms of hair attachment:

1 To weave the hair on weaving silks to form weft.
2 To knot the hair on to a net foundation.
3 To plant the hair into wax.
4 To punch graft the living hair root into the scalp.
5 To bind and sew false hair to growing hair, called hair extensions.
6 To lay hair on to the face and secure with spirit gum or latex.

In this book we cover 1, 2, 5 and 6; 3 and 4 require specialized knowledge.

9 Wig and postiche making

Measuring for wigs and postiche

Correct measurements of the head in order to make a wig will enable you to:

- make a wig yourself
- order a wig to sell to a client
- hire a wig of the correct size.

Wigs are worn today for a variety of reasons, as we have seen in Chapter 8:

- illness and disease which may have caused baldness
- theatre, television and stage
- fashion
- religious
- sign of office
- hair breakage
- burns
- scars.

Your client will fit into one of these categories, and you must establish which.

Remember that your attitude towards the client is important. You should be discreet, tactful, sympathetic and professional throughout. In particular, bald people may be self-conscious. Always find a suitable place to present the postiche.

Before you take the order for postiche, advise the client of the benefits and comparative costs of different types of postiche, as discussed in Chapter 8.

Synthetic postiche has the following characteristics:

- machine made, knotted or hand wefted
- cheaper than human hair
- immediately available
- adjustable to fit most sizes
- easy to maintain
- set in a definite style
- short life
- hot to wear.

Human hair has properties as follows:

- good fit, made to measure
- comfortable, cool to wear
- will last seven years or more
- higher servicing costs, needs professional maintenance
- change hairstyles and colour
- made to order.

Equipment required

Tape measure.
Gown.
Roll of tracing paper. Prepare paper beforehand (Figure 9.4): cut length 70 cm, width 30 cm; fold down the middle lengthwise, fold across the middle widthwise; open and leave flat.
Scissors.
Adhesive tape.
Dress-making pins.
Black felt tip pen.
Postiche order form (Figure 9.1).
Pencil or pen.

If client has hair, include:

Hair grips.
Elastic bands.
Elastic Alice band.
Dressing comb.
Tail comb.
Section hairdressing clips.

Tape measures

Measurements for postiche are taken with an ordinary tape measure. It is important that the same tape measure is used for drawing the pattern and measuring the pattern on to the wooden block (this is called mounting the wig). Tape measures tend to stretch with use. They can be checked against a steel rule. If you are not making the postiche, send the wigmaker the tape measure you have used as well as the paper pattern and order form.

Client's name ....

Address ....

....

Telephone: home.. work...

Order for: 1 wig ☐   2 wigs ☐   Hand-made ☐   Acrylic ☐   Hair-lace front ☐

Ordered by: NHS ☐   Private ☐   Theatre or media ☐

Measurements

	Measurements	Notes
Circumference (1 cm back centre front)		
Front to nape		
Ear to ear (front)		
Ear to ear (top)		
Temple to temple (back)		
Nape of neck (width of nape)		
Parting length		

Parting: left ☐   centre ☐   right ☐

distance from centre ....

Crown point ....

Natural break: left ☐   centre ☐   right ☐   crown ☐ ....

Abnormalities: (scalp ☐   bumps ☐   etc.)   ....

Wears: hearing aid ☐   glasses ☐   ....

Details of hair

A   Length: front   ....

temples   ....

crown   ....

nape   ....

B   Exact colour: pattern   ....
Enclose samples

C   Straight ☐   waved ☐
    Curly ☐   loose ☐   medium ☐   strong ☐

D   Full fringe

E   Weight of wig: light ☐   normal ☐   heavy ☐

F   Style: detailed notes

Drawings, picture or photo

Front   *Back*   *Side*

Foundation fitting   Date
_____

Cost ....   Client signature ....

Deposit ....   Date ....

Wig to be completed by ....   Date ....

Made by ....

Checked by ....

Dressed by ....

Figure 9.1   *Postiche order form*

Taking the measurements

Sit the client on a chair in front of a mirror in a suitable room, and put a gown on the client. Discuss with the client what he/she requires, as explained earlier, and start to fill in the order form (Figure 9.1). Before you start measuring, explain to the client what you are going to do.

If your client has hair then you must prepare the head first (see Chapter 7). Make sure the hairline is clearly visible; if it is not, agree the hairline with the client. This could be lightly marked in with a washable felt tip pen.

The measurements are as follows (see Figures 9.2, 9.3):

Circumference This is the total distance around the head. The angle is important; it can change because of a receding hairline. In most situations the circumference starts about 2 cm back from the centre front hairline.

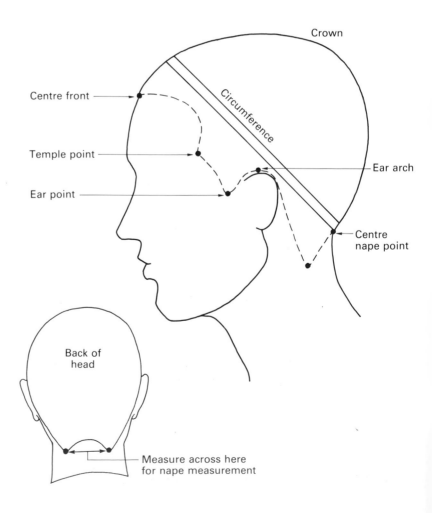

Figure 9.2 *Head measurement terminology*

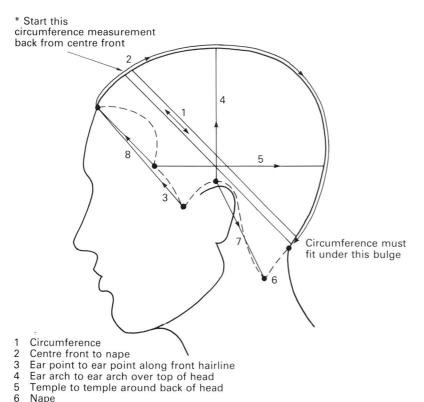

* Start this circumference measurement back from centre front

Circumference must fit under this bulge

1 Circumference
2 Centre front to nape
3 Ear point to ear point along front hairline
4 Ear arch to ear arch over top of head
5 Temple to temple around back of head
6 Nape
7 Ear arch to nape
8 Temple to temple front hairline

Figure 9.3 *Measurements for a wig*

Centre forehead (hairline) to nape   Begin at the centre of the exact hairline. Pass over the crown of the head to the centre of the nape. Ask the client to bend their head backwards and measure to this point.

Ear to ear, front   Begin at the left ear point. Bring the tape measure along the hairline to the right ear point.

Ear to ear, top   Begin at the left ear arch. Bring the tape measure over the top of the head to the right ear arch. Make sure you have a finger's width between ear and ear arch. Clearance of the ears is very important.

Temple to temple, back   Begin at the left temple. Travel around the back of the head (the tape measure must pass over the bulge of the head at the back) to the right temple.

Nape   Measure across the neck.

When the measurements have been completed and filled in correctly on the order form, you make the pattern.

Pattern making for a wig

The numbers in this procedure correspond to those in Figure 9.4:

1 Take the prepared piece of tracing paper.
2 Place the centre of the paper on the centre of the hairline (fold A).
3 Slide this paper centre back to where you started measuring the circumference from.
4 The centre fold line B you made on the paper now represents that circumference line. Take it round the head and pin it in the nape.
5 Check that the circumference line is in the right position all around the head.
6 Now trace the hairline on one side of the paper using the felt tip. Stop tracing just past the ear.
7 Remove paper.
8 Lie paper flat, with it folded in the middle fold (centre front). Pin in a few places to hold the paper still.
9 Now cut out the hairline shape, so that you are cutting both sides of the paper pattern together (C to D).
10 Only cut as far as behind the ears, because when you return the pattern to the head the nape will drop.
11 Place it back on the head, position correctly, pin nape paper.
12 Now trace one side only of the nape hairline.
13 Repeat 8 and 9 for the neck section only (cut E to F, G to H).
14 Place back on the head to check it is correct.

You now have an exact pattern of the hairline in order to make a wig (Figure 9.5). Complete the order form; the client's signature shows that it is an agreed contract for you to carry out the work.

The pattern can be used to make the following (Figure 9.6):

Transformation Worn with client's own hair.

Semi-transformation Cut pattern to fit this shape. Worn with client's own hair.

Wig Worn over baldness or client's own hair.

Semi-wig Worn over client's own hair. Does not have a nape.

Hair-lace front wig Worn over client's own hair.

Base for a head-dress Used for fitted head-dresses.

Natural hairline

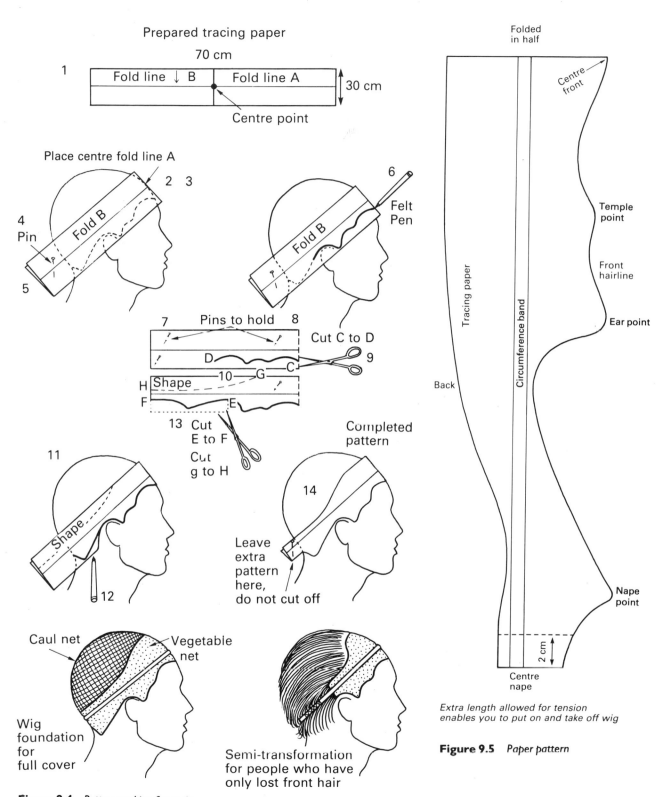

Figure 9.4 *Pattern making for a wig*

Figure 9.5 *Paper pattern*

Extra length allowed for tension enables you to put on and take off wig

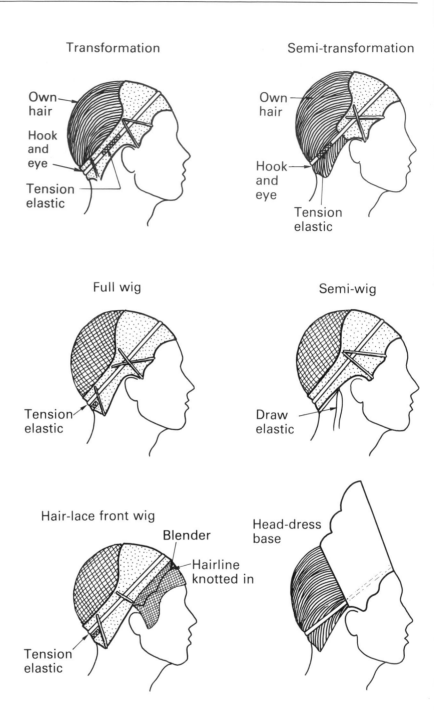

Transformation

Own hair

Hook and eye

Tension elastic

Semi-transformation

Own hair

Hook and eye

Tension elastic

Full wig

Tension elastic

Semi-wig

Draw elastic

Hair-lace front wig

Blender

Hairline knotted in

Tension elastic

Head-dress base

Figure 9.6 *Knotted foundations made from wig pattern: note different positions of tension elastics (Figure 8.7 included)*

To make a toupee template

The equipment required is the same as for making a pattern for a wig, with the addition of a polythene sheet/bag, a record card, a template order form and a black pen suitable for marking polythene.

Greet the client and show him to a suitable room. Gown him and sit him in front of a mirror. Discuss the exact requirements with the client, and start to fill in the order form (Figure 9.7). Note the style, the density of hair, the texture of hair and the length and degree of curl required.

Take a sample of hair from the back of the head. Take a few hairs from the side of the head. These samples are used for colour matching.

If the hairline is not clear, agree this line with the client before you start making the template. If the client frowns, this will show the lost hairline clearly. Take a water-based felt tip and lightly draw in the agreed hairline on the skin.

Numbers 1–5 in the following sequence correspond to those in Figure 9.8:

1 Take the polythene sheet and stretch it over the client's head, covering the bald area. Make sure you avoid covering the eyes, nose and mouth. Most people like to have an assistant to help hold the polythene down tight and still; if this is not possible, ask the client to help you. If you cannot find someone to practise on, use a plastic head-shaped block on a wig stand; you can draw in the area that would require the template.
2 Take adhesive tape and scissors. Lay strips of tape from front forehead to back of head. Continue to do this until bald area is covered.
3 Change direction with the tape: lay strips from side to side. Start at front forehead and travel to back of head. Make sure the tape overlaps the bald area.
4 Take the marker pen and draw in the outline of the bald area.
5 Now on the template also mark the positions in which the hair must lie for the required hairstyle. If it will need a parting, draw in now.
6 Make one more layer of adhesive tape over the marks to protect them.
7 Lift sheet off the head and cut out the drawn shape.
8 Place back on client's head and check fit. Trim if required.

Pad out the template for storage or postage. Check the hairstyle and hair colour again; remember that the front hairline is always lighter than the back of the head. Confirm the number of toupees, the price and the required dates. Complete the order form.

Note that most wigmakers recommend a fitting of foundations before they knot the hair in.

Client's name and reference number ....

....

Address ....

....

Requirements: toupee

<u>Measurements or template</u>

Before and after loss
photographs (if possible)

Required notes on measurements

Front ....

Side I ....

Side II ....

Back ....

<u>Reference to:</u>

<u>Style:</u> attach picture if possible

<u>Length of hair/colour:</u> samples if possible

<u>Density/texture</u> ....

<u>Degree of curl</u> ....

<u>Abnormalities</u> ....

<u>Partings length</u> .... <u>Position</u> ....

<u>Means of attachment</u> ....

Price quoted .... Client signature ....

Date ....

Date of order/fitting dates ....

Name of company/person ordering ....

Address ....

....

Ref. no ....

Figure 9.7 *Workroom order form for a toupee*

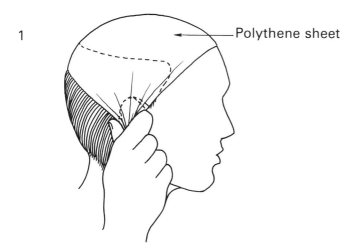

1 — Polythene sheet

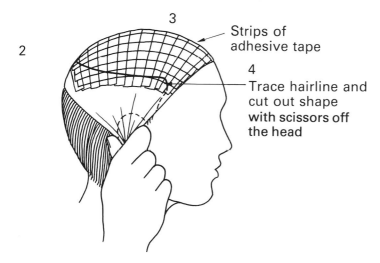

2

3 — Strips of adhesive tape

4 — Trace hairline and cut out shape **with scissors off the head**

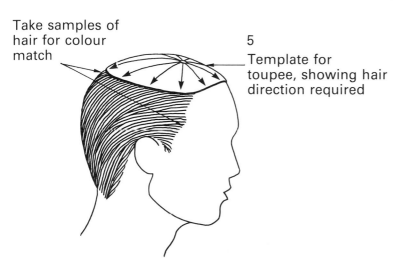

Take samples of hair for colour match

5 — Template for toupee, showing hair direction required

Figure 9.8 *Making a toupee template*

Plaster casting

This technique is useful when making a toupee. The cast can be personalized and stored for a particular client. It can be used in place of a wooden block when making the postiche.

Casts can also be used for making a false nose if one is required for a stage production.

1 Put protective gown on client.
2 Grease client's scalp and hair.
3 Make a cardboard crown which is topless but still has a high brim.
4 Place a large polythene sheet over client's scalp, so that it adheres to the grease.
5 Grease side away from scalp with petroleum jelly.
6 Place topless brim crown in position and grease inside it.
7 All gaps between should be plugged.
8 Mix dental grade of plaster of Paris and water together; follow instructions on packet.
9 Pour this mixture into rough formed by the sides of the crown and head.
10 Warn client that it will be heavy and warm.
11 Wait until it sets, then remove carefully.
12 Place into a box upside down. This is the negative cast.
13 Grease inside of negative cast.
14 Make up more dental plaster and pour into cast.
15 When set, carefully separate the casts.
16 Allow the positive cast to dry out for at least a week.
17 While it is fresh, set in points for bracing; patterns can be traced directly on to the plaster. Mark in name or number as required.
18 Varnish positive cast for protection.

Assessments

1 What kind of attitude should you have when seeing a client who has come to order a wig?
2 What is the difference between a full wig and a semi-wig?
3 How do you prepare your client?
4 What kind of room is suitable to take measurements for a wig?
5 List the six main measurements for a wig.
6 What do you take measurements with?

7 What must you fill in when taking an order?
8 Name four important facts that you must establish about this order.
9 Why is a photograph helpful to the wigmaker?
10 How do we ensure we have the perfect fit?
11 What is the difference between a transformation and a semi-transformation?
12 How do you make a toupee template?
13 What marks do you make on the template?
14 How important are hair samples?
15 What length of tracing paper would you prepare for a wig?
16 Draw out a wig pattern shape and label the main points.
17 Name five reasons why wigs are worn today.
18 Name three things that correct measuring for postiche will enable you to do.
19 Make a paper pattern for a wig.
20 Make a paper pattern for semi-transformation.
21 Make a template for a toupee.
22 Make a template for a chignon.

Keep the templates from 19–22 safely; they will be required for examination.

Making a wig

I have included this because I believe that everyone who is involved in this type of work should make one wig.

There are different ways of making a wig. It depends on the type of life you expect the wig to have. This in turn affects your choice of foundation and quality of hair. Briefly, you can divide hand-made wigs into three categories:

Heavy net foundation with galloon   An everyday wig. It can be used for theatre, film and television as well.

Very light net foundation without galloon   This is very popular for theatres, film and television. It is very light to wear. It has a hair-lace front.

Very light front net with heavy back net foundation and galloon   This is used for theatre, film and television. It is heavier to wear than the second type. It has a hair-lace front.

Measurements and mounting

You have already covered measurement taking for a wig. You have filled in a postiche order form. You have made a paper pattern for a wig. When a pattern is cut, not all the measurements are used. The remaining measurements are checked when mounting.

Prepare for mounting as follows:

1 Take the circumference measurement and choose the most suitable block, one that is 2 cm larger than this measurement around the circumference.
2 Check centre front nape measurements. This will give you the correct depth of the wig.
3 Check ear-to-ear measurement over the top of the head. This will give you the height of the head.
4 Mark these positions with a piece of chalk.

You can damp the pattern before you mount it. Then find the approximate hairline position. Place the centre front of the pattern on the centre front of the block. Run the pattern around the block to conform with the chalk marks. Check all the measurements now. Secure with adhesive tape or block points.

Continue mounting as in the following sections.

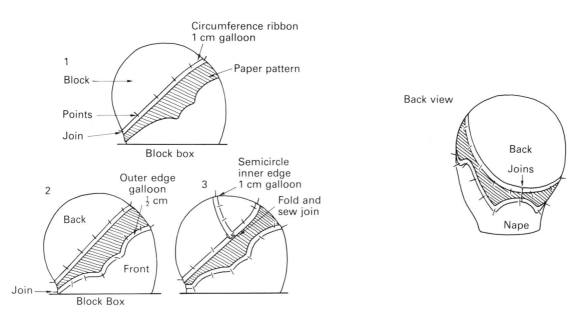

Figure 9.9 *Pointing galloons*

Galloons (silk ribbons)

The numbers in the following correspond to those on Figure 9.9:

1 Take a 1 cm wide galloon and encircle the head in the circumference position. Start and finish in the nape. Leave enough galloon to sew the ends together. Fasten the galloon with points. Use as few points as possible.
2 Take a 1/2 cm wide galloon, encircle the hairline starting in the nape. Fasten galloon with as few points as possible. It is best to curve the galloon whenever possible; try not to make pleats. Cut off the galloon at the centre back, leaving enough for a neatly sewn join.
3 Take the 1 cm wide galloon and form a semicircle over the top part of the head. Fold the ends of the galloon on to the circumference band and sew. Use points sparingly to hold the galloons in place.

Foundation sewing technique

1 Use a sewing silk that matches the colour of the net and galloon.
2 Treat the silk with beeswax before use.
3 Use a neat stitch, run and fell seam for joins and a hemming stitch for runs.
4 Use a finger shield (Figure 9.10) for picking up the point of the needle. The thimble protects your finger from the needle.

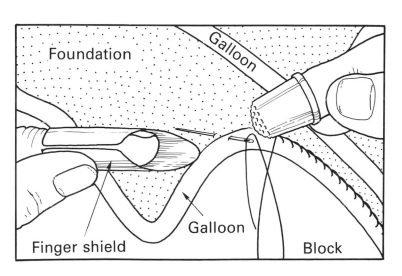

Figure 9.10 *Finger shield and thimble*

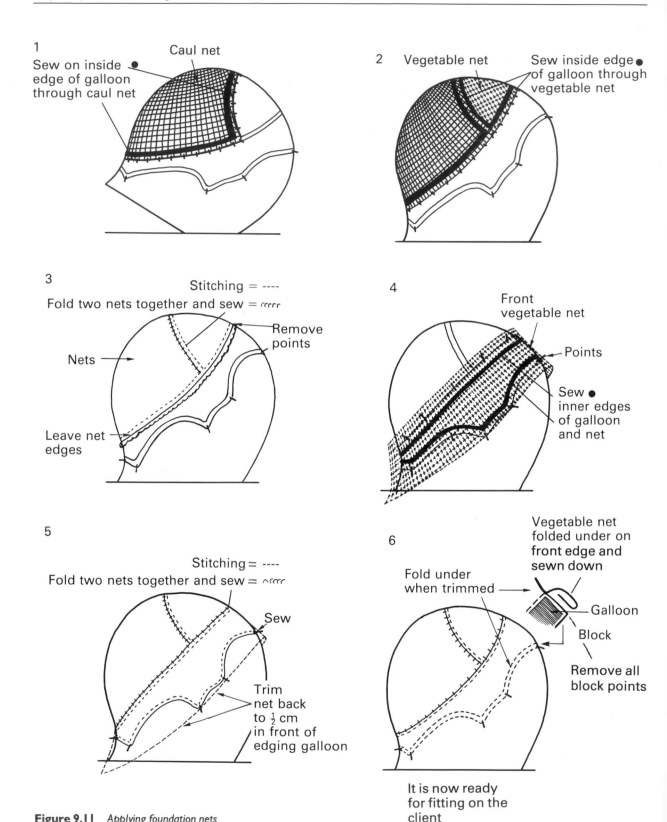

Figure 9.11 *Applying foundation nets*

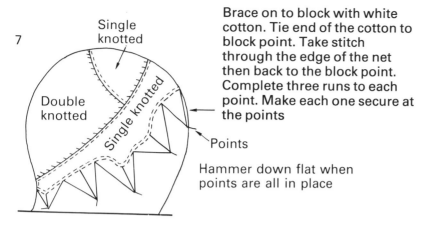

7

Single knotted

Double knotted

Single knotted

Points

Brace on to block with white cotton. Tie end of the cotton to block point. Take stitch through the edge of the net then back to the block point. Complete three runs to each point. Make each one secure at the points

Hammer down flat when points are all in place

Foundation net

Caul net

Measure on the block, then cut out the amount you require (always allow slightly more for joins) (Figure 9.11, part 1).

Wet the caul net and place in position on the block. The block points will be standing up, so you can hook the caul net on to these. You may have to adjust some of the points. Use a hammer to knock the points down sideways. They should face outwards and hold the net in position.

Take a needle and prepared sewing silk plus a finger shield and commence sewing through the caul net into the inner edge of the circumference galloon. Sew along this edge using a small neat hemming stitch. The run of the stitch is on the top of the caul net: remember that this is the hair side, so the sewing must not show on the underside.

Make sure there is enough caul net to cover the galloon and to make a hem later on.

Vegetable net

Cut a piece of vegetable net that will cover the top semicircle (Figure 9.11, part 2). It must be larger than the actual size because of the hemming. Wet this net, place it in position on to the block and point it; remember to remove any points underneath the net first. Sew the inner edge of the galloon and net together with neat hemming stitch.

Measure the amount of vegetable net you require to encircle the head (part 4 of figure). Cut this out and wet the net. Fold the net in the middle and place it on the centre front; point in position. Smooth the net around the block to the nape. Overlap in the nape for the joint. Remember to put out points under the net as you work around the block; replace with new ones. Sew the inner edge of the vegetable net and galloon, then sew the inner edge of the vegetable net and hairline galloon.

Now fold and trim net that overlaps. Fold net edges neatly together into a flat seam point and sew down (part 5 of figure). When you have sewn the seams, you can remove the block points.

You now have to prepare the hairline edge for sewing. Remove all the block points along the hairline. Take a pair of scissors and trim the vegetable net back to about 1/4 cm (part 6 of figure). Turn this under between the galloon to make a hem that goes all round the hairline. Sew with a neat hemming stitch. You can take the wig off and hold it in your hands to sew if you want to, as all the points should have been removed by now. When you have sewn all the hairline, return the wig to the block.

Make arrangements for your client to have a foundation fitting. If alterations are required, it is best to do them before bracing and knotting (part 7 of the figure).

Bracing

We will now brace the wig on to the block ready to knot the hair in. We brace a wig so that we can remove all the points from the block and in so doing protect our hands from catching on them while knotting.

To brace, place block points opposite each of the salient points of the wig, 3 cm away and 5 cm apart all round the hairline. When all the points are in position, prepare a needle with long white thread, and brace as shown in Figure 9.11, part 7. Then knock outside points down flat.

Knotting techniques

Single knotting

The numbers in the following correspond to Figure 9.12:

1 Place your section of hair into the drawing mats/brushes with the roots facing you.
2 Take a knotting hook with holder size 2 and hold it in your right hand like a pen, with the hook facing up. For speed, some hold it as in Figure 9.12(3).

3 Draw a few hairs out from the mats and fold over the root ends to form a loop. Hold the loop with your left hand between thumb and forefinger.

4 Slide the hook into and under one strand of net foundation. Slide the hook in on its side: when it comes up, turn it to stick out. Take your left hand with the hair loop over to the hook. Let the hook catch one or two hairs.

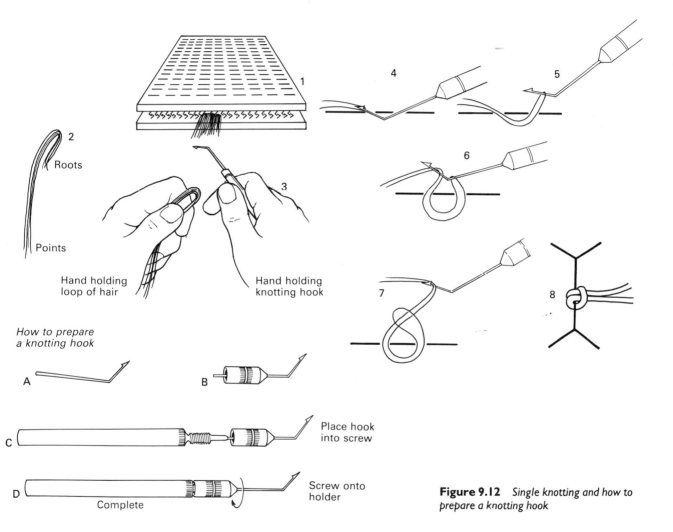

How to prepare a knotting hook

Figure 9.12 *Single knotting and how to prepare a knotting hook*

5 Draw the hook backwards and sideways under the strand of net foundation, drawing it out only a little way.

6 Let the hook catch the hair that has not gone through the net.

7 This time take the hair through the hair loop you have just made.

8 Pull the hair right through to make a knot.

Some practice is necessary to achieve the required dexterity of working with both hands together. You must remember to keep the tension even between both hands so that the hair does not become slack.

Double knotting

Make a single knot first. Then repeat the process (Figure 9.12, parts 6–8) to make two knots instead of one (Figure 9.13). This adds strength to the knot.

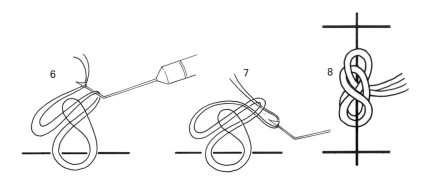

Figure 9.13 *Double knotting (repeats sequence 6–8 in Figure 9.12)*

Assessments

1 For practice, single knot an inch square of vegetable net – try every other hole first.
2 For practice, double knot an inch square of caul net – try every other hole and every other line first.

Knotting the wig

Preparation

You will need a small box to place your block in when working, in order to keep the block still.

Always try to sit upright to a bench or table. Make sure you have a good light to work by. You may find you need glasses for this close work. It is best to get a pair rather than to suffer eye strain and possible headaches.

Refer to your order form and check hairstyle requirements. Prepare quantity, colour and curl of hair to those requirements.

The types of knotting required are:

Single knotting   Used on vegetable net (foundation net).

Point knotting   Knot points of the hair first and cut off the root end. This keeps the natural curl of the hair. Use for toupees.

Double knotting   Used on the caul net.

Under knotting   Form of single knotting used on galloon for front hairline. Used to hide the edge.

Figure 9.11, part 6, suggests a basic knotting arrangement for the wig constructed.

Start the knotting by finely and closely single knotting all around the edge of the hairline. (This can be point knotted if short curls are required.)

Then start in the nape and work up the head, going from side to side. When you are near the hairline, knot the hair in every hole; otherwise knot every other hole and every other line. The style of the wig will indicate where it is necessary to place the hair more thickly.

Follow the natural growth of the hair when knotting, and keep your work close and fine. Figure 9.14 shows some of the options for direction knotting. If the hairstyle has no parting, the centre front section back to the crown of the wig must be cross knotted, that is one row to the right and the next row to the left. This stops any gaps appearing and makes the hair stand up off the foundation.

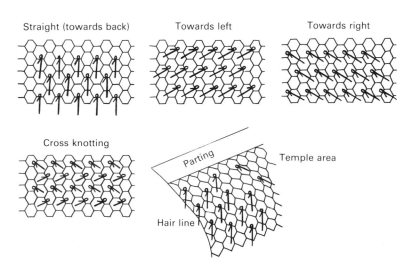

Figure 9.14   *Direction knotting*

Under knotting

When you have filled in all the hair on top of the foundation, you cut the bracing and remove the wig. Take a malleable block of the correct size. Turn the wig inside out and pin it on to the malleable block. Pin the front hairline securely.

Start under knotting just past the centre front hairline edge. Knot one row all the same way towards the ear point. Turn the block around and repeat, travelling in the opposite direction towards the other ear point.

Repeat this until you have completed two rows. The under knotting is knotted into the bound edge of the galloon. It is knotted parallel to the edge of the hairline. Link one single knot into the next like a chain. This forms a neat continuous line which conceals the edge of the foundation when it is combed in with the hair on top of the foundation.

Springs

Positional springs

These can be made of metal, wire or plastic. Springs are used to hold the shape of the salient points of the wig. If springs were not fitted, the front foundation would roll back during combing or brushing. Ready-made plastic springs are not as effective as the others.

We cross and bend the temple and ear positional springs to make a slight curve which holds these salient points close fitting to the head. They are not required on hair-lace front wigs.

Figure 9.15 shows how to make positional springs. Figure 9.16 shows spring positions.

Tension springs

These can be made of metal spring or elastic strip. Elastic strips are more popular with clients because they are soft to the head. However, they do need renewing frequently because they can perish during dry cleaning.

The tension springs are placed at the back of the wig (Figure 9.16) on the galloon. They are used to take up the slack of the wig, which enables you to take the wig on and off easily as well as offer a tight fit to the head.

Figure 9.17 shows how to make tension springs.

1 Measure each position for springs required (see Figure 9.16))
2 Cut fine watch-spring to size
3 Rub ends into curve on hard stone
4 Cover ends with fabric plaster

5 Enclose springs in thin waterproof material, e.g. oiled silk, fish skin.
   This protects from rusting. Fold ends in and stitch or wind cotton around

6 Wind cotton around to hold secure

7 Cut wide galloon longer than spring

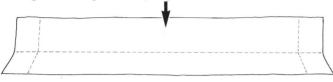

Fold end in and
stitch

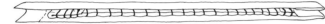

8 Proceed to sew into bind edge with small stitches all the way around

You will need seven positional springs for wig without a parting: *See Figure 9.16 for positions*
A parting requires a positional spring each side of it

Positional springs can be sewn to the wig on the hair side of foundation before hair is knotted, or after the wig has been made on inside of the foundation. It depends on required use of wig; remember springs often need replacing

Figure 9.15   *Making positional springs*

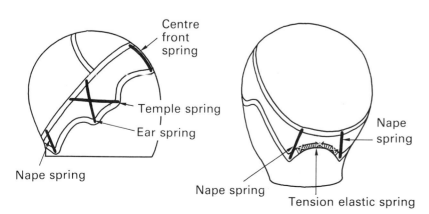

Centre
front
spring

Temple spring

Ear spring

Nape spring

Nape
spring

Nape spring

Tension elastic spring

Figure 9.16   *Spring positions*

1   Sew piece of elastic strip to wide galloon

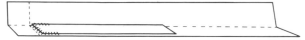

2   Fold galloon ends in and sew along bind edge

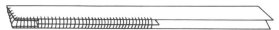

As far as end of elastic strip. Knot cotton securely

3   Now push sewn galloon back, revealing end of elastic

4   Take this end of elastic and stretch to sew at other end of galloon, allowing enough galloon to turn in

5   Fold and sew galloon over end of elastic

6   Sew remaining edge of galloon to conceal elastic

7

Tubular galloon can be used, which is much easier. This can be sewn to nape of wig with elastic loose inside

Elastic can then be used like drawstring to adjust on client

You can just sew elastic strip on its own on to nape galloon. Hold in place with herringbone stitch. Then pull up open end of elastic to take up elastic slack. Then sew down securely

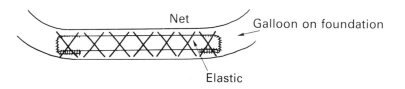

Figure 9.17   *Making tension elastic spring*

Dressing the wig

When you have completed all the work, place the wig securely on a clean malleable block. Block up the wig and dress it as described in Chapter 10.

Partings

A parting is the line drawn on the scalp by the point tooth of a comb, dividing the hair.

The details required for a parting pattern are:

- distance from centre forehead to centre of parting (space)
- width of parting
- length of parting
- position of parting, i.e. right, left or centre
- other details, e.g. slope of head, i.e. parting line goes up towards the crown or away from it.

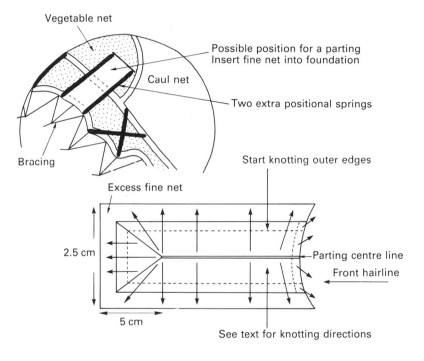

Top view of finished knotted parting

Front

Figure 9.18 *Making simple flat knotted parting*

Knotted parting

This is an indefinite line dividing one hair direction from another. It is sometimes called a knotted break point. It is frequently used on cheaper types of postiche.

You may be required to put in a knotted parting on your wig or hair piece. This is how you do it (Figure 9.18):

1 Draw a paper pattern to size and place it in the position you require it.
2 You should be knotting on fine see-through net with a fine knotting hook.
3 Start from the outer edges of the parting.
4 Knot with single knotting in the directions marked. Knot every other hole and every other row for three rows.
5 Knot every hole and every row on the remainder of the parting.
6 Remember to keep the front of the parting line knotted as a natural hairline. Stagger fine knots for two rows.

A small parting is required as an examination work sample (5 cm × 2.5 cm) for City and Guilds. It can of course be set in a larger knotted hair piece (Figure 9.19).

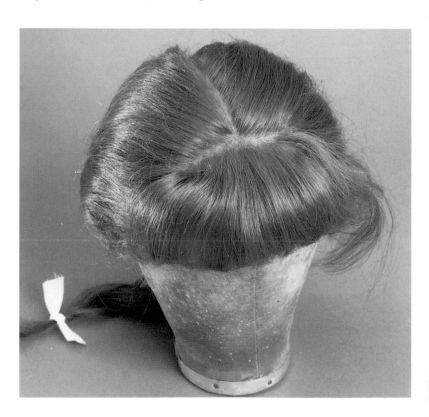

Figure 9.19 *Knotted parting*

Hair-lace partings (fine nylon net)

This is a variation of a knotted parting. Fine net is set into the parting space. The hair is knotted a single hair at a time on to the fine net. The parting is then sometimes lined with parting silk.

Some knotters knot the hair all forward and then comb it back and divide it into a parting. This gives the hair lift and is more suitable for modern fuller hairstyles.

This is much finer work as less hair is used.

Drawn-through partings

With these the hair is drawn through a silk cloth to imitate the natural scalp. There are two methods: English and French.

English method

1 Take measurements required.
2 Cut a pattern to the exact size; use thin card.
3 Pin this pattern on to a malleable block.
4 Cut a piece of etamine gauze (a white net with square holes) on foundation net about 2 cm larger than the pattern.
5 Pin the net over the pattern.
6 Using single knotting, start to knot about 1 cm back from the front. Knot the hair forward. Knot finely in every hole and every line. Cut the roots off as close to the net as possible. Use size 0 or 00 parting hooks.
7 When the knotting is completed, comb all the hair towards the front.
8 Cut a piece of silk about 3 cm larger all round than the pattern.
9 Pin the silk over the knotted area securely.
10 Start at the back edge using your fine knotting hook. Insert it through the silk to pick up one or two hairs. Draw out the hook and the hairs. Repeat this process row by row until you have drawn all the knotted hair through the silk. If the silk does tear, it can be pulled off and replaced with a new piece, so you can start again.
11 When all the hair is drawn through, take the parting off the malleable block.
12 Trim net back to the knotting and pattern edge.
13 Make a neat hem of the parting silk and sew all round underneath the parting.

14 This is now ready to be inserted into a hair piece.

Any gaps on the parting silk around the edges may be filled in with single knotting after the insertion.

French method

For the French method the knotting and drawing-through work is completed in one exercise. Repeat the English method 1–4. Then proceed as follows:

5 Cut the parting silk and pin at the front edge only.
6 Pass the knotting hook through the silk in front of the net.
7 Knot the hair to the gauze or net, then withdraw the hair and hook through the same hole in the parting silk as you entered by. The net is visible through the silk, and this helps the placing of the hook.
8 Pin down the silk as the work advances.
9 When the parting area is complete, finish as in the English method 11–14.

The marking of drawn-through partings in most workrooms is a very specialized job, executed by experienced and much practised postiche makers.

In some fashion wigs made of synthetic fibre or real hair reduced by acids, the drawn-through work is used for the whole middle front to crown areas. The rest of the wig is made of machine weft. This type of postiche is called a 'combination wig' because it mixes hand-made work with machine-made work.

Making a knotted chignon

Preparation

Receive the client and discuss the size and shape of chignon. Fill in the order form (Figure 9.20). Take hair samples.

Agree with the client the exact position for the chignon to be worn. Measure and cut out the pattern on stiff paper. Position it on the head to see if it is the right size.

For the 301 City and Guilds wigmaking examination you are required to make one knotted hair piece. The chignon is the smallest one you can make (do not make it smaller than 8 cm diameter). Cut a suitable pattern.

For client, proceed as follows.

Client's name ....

Address ....

....

Requirements: chignon round
                           nape

Measurements

Area to be covered: vertically ....

                         horizontally ....

Tried on client: moulded to shape..

Strengthen outline of pattern with adhesive tape ....

                                                 ....

Indicate on pattern direction of hair   ....

                                               ....

Means of attachment:

Reference to

Style required ....

Length of hair/colour (sample) ....

Density/texture ....

Price quoted..   Client signature ....

Date of order..   Date...

Name of company ....

Address ....

Name of operator...

Figure 9.20 *Chignon order form*

Mounting

1 Wet the paper pattern and place it on to a wooden block in the position that it is to be worn.
2 Take 1 cm galloon and carefully point around the edge of the pattern with block points. Make sure you have no pleats in the galloon. Leave enough galloon to fold together and sew in a net join. Leave the points standing up.
3 Cut out a colour matching piece of vegetable net, larger than required.
4 Carefully place the net down on top of the points and pull through to the pattern. Be careful not to tear the net. You can move some of the points if required.
5 Tap the points down and away from the centre with a hammer. This leaves the net flat and smooth to the block.

6 Take the prepared sewing silk, finger shield, needle and thimble and start to sew through the net, picking up the bound inner edge of the underlying galloon. Sew with hemming stitch, with the run of the stitch on the hair side. Complete the inner circle.

7 Take the block points out with pliers and trim the net back to about 1/2 cm from the outer edge of the galloon.

8 Fold this edge back between the top net and the galloon all round the circumference.

9 Sew with fine blanket stitch or hemming stitch.

10 Measure the diameter of the chignon and make two positional springs to sew underneath the foundation to hold its shape. These can be attached on the hair side before knotting.

11 Point back on to the block and brace.

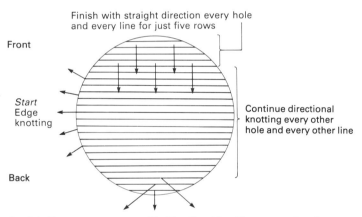

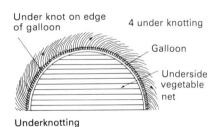

Figure 9.21 *One way of knotting a chignon*

Knotting

1 Knot with single knots in every hole all round the edge of the circumference (Figure 9.21).

2 Work in lines starting from the edge. Knot every other hole and every other line with directional knotting. Finish with a section of straight knotting, every hole and every line.

3 Cut the bracing, remove the block points and reverse side to pin on to a malleable block.

4 Under knot two rows of single knotting around the circumference on the outer galloon bound edge.

5 A small postiche comb or clip should be sewn on to the under foundation for attachment.

6 Place back on to malleable block and secure with pins. Then damp down hair and dress as required.

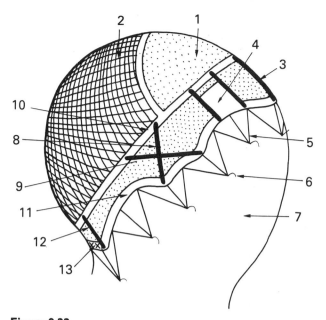

Figure 9.22

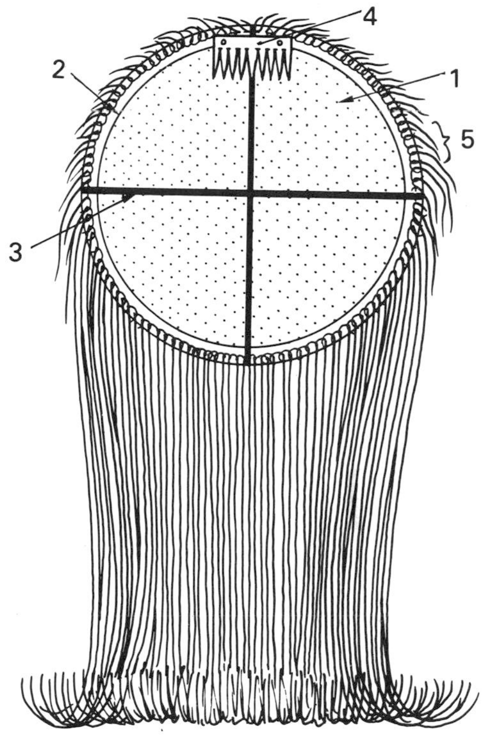

Figure 9.23

Assessments

1 When beginning to mount the wig, what do we place on the block after the pattern?
2 How do we secure it to the block?
3 Name two foundation nets used in wigmaking.
4 How is the net secured to the block?
5 How do we prepare sewing silks?
6 What tool do we use to help pick up the end of the needle when sewing in the foundation?
7 What do we make to hold the salient points of a wig firm, so that the foundation net will not roll back?
8 Explain how to make a positional spring.
9 What do we make to take up the slack on a wig foundation?
10 Explain what bracing is.
11 What kind of knotting do you use on vegetable net?
12 What kind of knotting do you use on caul net?
13 Where do we use underknotting?
14 Name the parts labelled in Figure 9.22 (1–13).
15 Name the parts labelled in Figure 9.23. Name this postiche (1–6).

10 Cleaning, dressing and maintaining postiche

Dry cleaning postiche

If you wish to restyle a wig it must be made with real hair and usually hand knotted. This wig must be dry cleaned first.

The hand washing of synthetic and machine weft wigs is covered at the end of this chapter.

Equipment

Two plastic washing-up bowls.
Funnel and filter paper.
One can of industrial wig cleaner.
One empty can.
One washing line in open air.
Wooden clothes-pegs.
Well ventilated room or back garden.

Precautions

Do not smoke while cleaning wigs.
Do not clean near any inflammable substances.
Do not dry in or on anything hot or warm.
Wig cleaner is a health hazard for people with heart or lung conditions.

Method

In well ventilated room or back garden:

1 Remove all hair slides and hair grips.
2 Pour industrial cleaner into plastic bowl.
3 Take dirty wig, turn inside-out and place into cleaner. *Do not rub foundation*: just squeeze the wig gently, several times.
4 Take wig from this bowl and place it in the empty bowl *to drip*. (If, however, the wig is *very* dirty, pour fresh cleaning spirit over the wig again and repeat the process: leave to soak).

5 Return to first bowl, and pour this cleaning spirit through a filter paper placed in the funnel back into the empty tin. Screw lid tightly on to tin, because spirit evaporates very quickly and it's expensive.

6 Return to wig and remove from bowl. Take the wig and hang it up on a washing line with a clothes-peg. It will dry in a matter of minutes.

7 Clear up the bowls. Store tins of industrial spirit in a cold safe place until further use. *Never* throw cleaning spirit down the drain or anywhere else. You must take it to the local tip, well labelled.

8 The wig will be dry now.

Blocking up a wig for setting and postiche dressing

In order not to damage the wig, you must first measure the circumference to find out what size head it is. Then find a malleable block that is the same size head.

Equipment

Malleable block (circumference size to be found on the base).
Wig stand.
Box of postiche pins (for setting). These are steel pins 4 to 5½ cm long.
Box of dress-making pins (blocking-up pins). These are pins 3 cm long.
Bowl of hot water.
Dressing comb.
Tail comb.
Tape.
Rollers of various sizes.
Setting lotion.
Box of hair grips and hair pins.
Hair dryer or postiche oven.
Paper pads (crushed wet paper dried into shapes like shoulder pads).
Two towels.
Polythene bag large enough to cover the malleable block. It protects the malleable canvas and wig foundation, and speeds drying.
Hair water spray.
Conditioner.

If you are going to tint, perm or bleach this wig, you would also require the necessary materials. However, only attempt this if you are a qualified hairdresser. See later in this chapter.

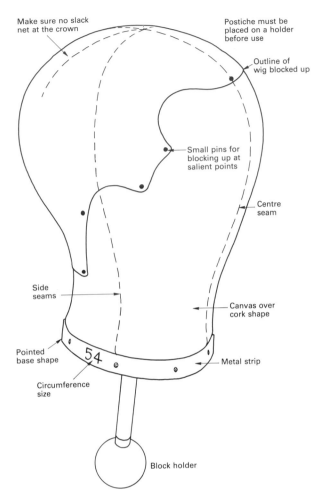

Figure 10.1 *Malleable block for setting and dressing: wig position usually with pointed base at back of block, but can be whatever gives best fit*

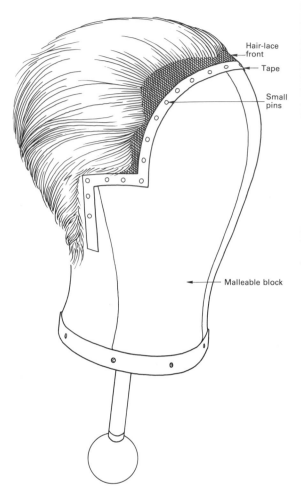

Figure 10.2 *Blocking up hair-lace front. Use small dress-making pins, not postiche pins: lift tape to remove pins*

Method

Refer to Figure 10.1. See also Figures 10.2 and 10.3.

1 Place malleable block on to wig stand.
2 Prepare block first by covering with polythene bag and pinning the polythene into the base.
3 Turn the wig inside out.
4 Find the centre front positional spring; there may be a postiche comb sewn in.
5 Place the centre front of the wig on to the centre seam of the malleable block.

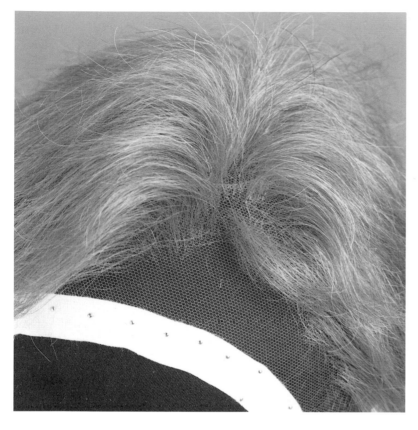

Figure 10.3 *Blocking up hair-lace front*

6 Turn the wig to bring it over the crown of the block. Pull down the ear points, one each side of the block.
7 Pull the nape of the wig down on to the back of the block.
8 Check that the front and ear points are in the right positions; correct if not.
9 Check for slack. If there is slack, pad out or find a better fitting malleable block.
10 Take blocking-up pins and place as follows (Figure 10.1):
   (a) Place one in the centre front.
   (b) Place one each side in the ear points.
   (c) Place one each side at the temples.
   (d) Give wig a firm pull down into the nape and pin both nape points.
   (e) Pin down any slack areas carefully.
   If you always follow this sequence it will be easier to remove the wig after it has been dressed.

It is essential to keep the wig foundation fitting as closely as possible to the malleable block without stretching it. This is because we are going to wet the hair and foundation. A tight fitting prevents the knots of the knotted hair becoming loose when swollen with water. The foundation will not shrink because it is on the right size of block. Furthermore, if the foundation net is tightly up against the block then we cannot catch and tear it easily while brushing and combing the wig.

Combing a wig

When you are certain that the wig is blocked up correctly, you can start to set it. First the wig needs to be combed out.

Take a large dressing comb and start to comb the hair from the points up to the roots. If it's a short wig this will be done quickly; the longer the hair, the more work is involved. Work in this way:

1 Start at the base of the nape, comb up to the crown, stop.
2 Starting at the base of the left ear point, comb up to the temple, stop.
3 Repeat for the right ear.
4 Start at the crown, comb forward to the front forehead.
5 Finish by combing from the front to the nape.

Dressing wigs

The most important rule for dressing any wig is that you must conceal the foundation hairline. Wigs are made with under knotting. The under knotting consists of a few lines of hair hand-knotted on the underside of the wig foundation. This hair comes out from underneath the edge and combs back into the hair knotted on the top side of the wig. This effect does soften the edge but still looks unnatural most of the time. The setting of the wig, therefore, has to provide a natural line that conceals the edge of the wig.

There are many hairstyles. I will give you examples of dressing a short wig with a day style and a more complicated long historical wig. I have tried to show a range of wig dressing techniques because wig dressing is different from hairdressing.

Postiche pins are used instead of clips because they are easy to place into the malleable block and do not damage the foundation or mark the hair.

Comb the hair exactly where you require it to be in the style. It will not change after it has been set.

When setting long hair, dress the hair up into the style and use tape to hold the weight of the hair in place. This will enable you to set or dress the points. When this is dry, do *not* take the long hair down; just dress the loose end areas.

Short hairstyle

Refer to Figure 10.4. See also Figure 10.5.

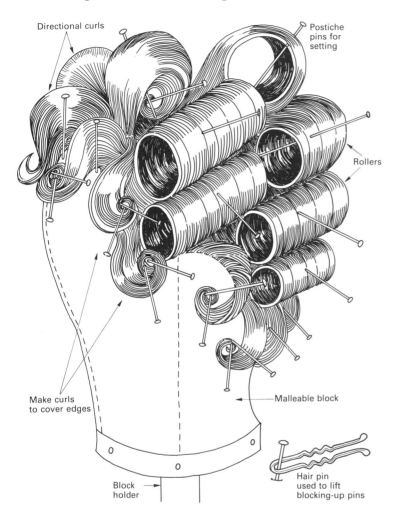

Figure 10.5 *Dressing wig with short hairstyle*

Figure 10.4 *Dressing wig with short hairstyle*

1 Correctly block up the wig.
2 Place towel on the table around the base of the stand.
3 Comb the wig out as described in the previous section.
4 Wet the wig with a large sponge soaked in hot water, or with a spray.
5 Comb the wig into hairstyle shape.
6 Section off front hairline hair.
7 Make directional curls to match the hairstyle. Hold these curls in place with postiche pins.

8 If the hairstyle has a directional divide (top front, for example), continue to use directional barrel curls instead of rollers.

9 Use rollers of the right proportion over the crown and back of the head. Hold these with postiche pins.

10 Do *not* use rollers on the edges of any wigs. Always keep the edge of the foundation flat to conceal it. A full style can always be dressed over this concealment afterwards.

11 Make flat curls in the nape and around the ears.

12 When you have completed the pli, place a hair net over the wig. Place it into a postiche oven to dry slowly overnight, or under a hair dryer. An airing cupboard will do.

13 When dry, remove net and allow to cool down before dressing out.

14 Remove all postiche pins and rollers carefully.

15 Take a small brush and start to brush in the neck, work up to the front hairline.

16 Pour a little brilliantine on to the palms of your hands, then run your hands through the hair. Always put brilliantine on the *back* of the wig first.

17 You can now back comb the roots a little to give lift, or just comb over the sides.

18 If you place the hair net back over the wig it will remove static electricity. Give the wig a light spray of lacquer and leave it on the block.

19 When the wig is required, use a thick type of hair pin to help ease the short blocking-up pins out of the block. This avoids pushing your fingers through the net (see Figure 10.4).

Long hairstyle

Refer to Figure 10.6. See also Figure 10.7.

1 Correctly block up the wig.
2 Correctly comb out the long hair.
3 Wet the hair well.
4 Decide on the style and work out the sequence of dressing.
5 Divide the hair into sections.
6 Work on the front hairline section first.
7 Make centre parting.
8 Take out short front edge hair.
9 Take out long piece of hair for ear ringlet.
10 Comb front wave movements into shape and hold each side with tape and pins (labelled A on Figure 10.6).
11 Comb crown smooth and hold with tape (labelled B).

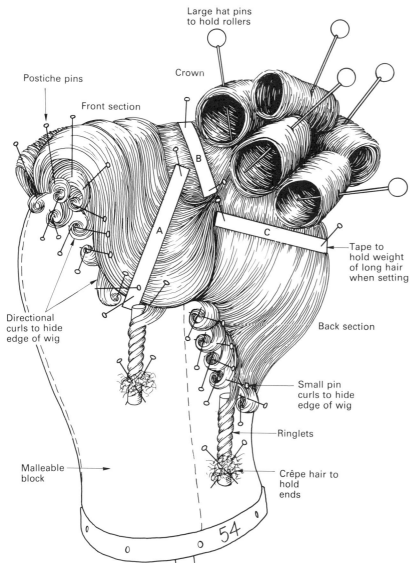

Large hat pins
to hold rollers

Crown

Postiche pins

Front section

B

A

C

Tape to
hold weight
of long hair
when setting

Directional
curls to hide
edge of wig

Back section

Small pin
curls to hide
edge of wig

Ringlets

Malleable
block

Crêpe hair to
hold
ends

54

Figure 10.6 *Dressing wig with long hairstyle*

Figure 10.7 *Dressing wig with long hairstyle*

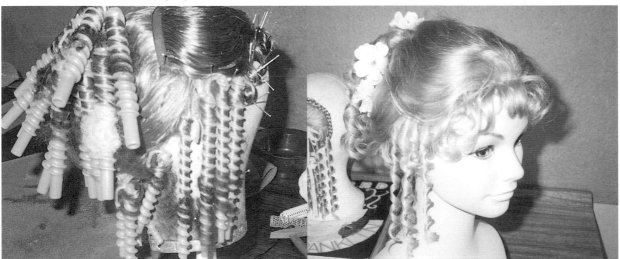

In pli

Dressed out

12 Turn the block round at an angle and comb all the hair at the back up towards the crown. Hold this with tape (labelled C).

13 The short hair at the nape will fall down. You can remove a long piece of hair for a ringlet.

14 Section the hair now on top of the crown into smaller sections to roll up on to rollers. Secure with hat pins or postiche pins.

15 Return to the front of the wig and make the directional pin curls to conceal the edge of the wig.

16 Continue down into the nape.

17 Finish by making the ringlets. Remember to wind from the roots to the points. Use setting lotion and make very smooth. Do *not* comb out when dry. They will last a long time. You can use setting lotion for any hairstyle; it does help with the setting and the length of the set's life.

18 Cover the set with a large net. Dry in postiche oven on slow heat for several hours, or use a hair dryer.

19 When dry, remove from oven and allow to cool. Remove the net.

20 Remove tape A and postiche pins on the front edge.

21 Take large dressing comb and carefully comb through this section to soften it only. You cannot comb the points because they are still fastened. Secure now with hair grips.

22 Remove tape B and repeat with comb. Secure with hair grips.

23 Remove postiche pins in the nape and remove tape C. Comb through hair up to rollers, secure with hair grips.

24 Remove rollers one at a time and comb through each section.

25 Arrange these curls and fix with hair grips or hair points. Lacquer a little.

26 Return to hairline, and comb each little curl and replace.

27 Finish by removing the ringlet sticks carefully. Do not comb the ringlets.

28 The wig is now ready to be worn. You should leave it on the block until required. Cover with tissue paper to protect it from dust.

Figures 10.8 and 10.9 show some other ideas for long hairstyles.

Figure 10.8 *Wigs with long historical hairstyles*

Figure 10.9 *Wig with long modern hairstyle*

White and pale wigs

If the wigs you are cleaning and dressing are white or pale coloured, you must take extra care as follows.

Cleaning

Clean separately from other postiche to avoid possible discoloration, such as from a wig that has had a colour rinse. Always use fresh cleaning spirit.

Blocking up

Use a clean malleable block or cover one with a clean polythene sheet or bag. Make sure the blocking-up pins are silver plated and are not rusty.

Setting

Make sure the brushes, combs and postiche pins are clean. With white wigs, a little blue rinse may be added to the setting water.

Drying

Cover the wigs with hair nets and some tissue paper. This prevents any discoloration from heat. Do *not* make the postiche oven too hot.

Assessments

1 What do you use to dry clean wigs with?
2 Name two precautions when dry cleaning wigs.
3 Explain how to dry clean a wig.
4 Before blocking up a wig in order not to damage it, what must you do?
5 Why do we use dress-making pins when blocking up?
6 How do we protect malleable blocks from discoloration and damage when setting wigs?
7 Explain how to put a wig on to a malleable block.
8 Give three reasons why it is important to block up a wig correctly.

9 What is the correct way to comb a long-haired wig when it is first placed on a block for dressing?
10 When setting wigs, what is the most important area to conceal?
11 How would you do this?
12 What do you use to hold curls and rollers in place?
13 If you are setting long hair, what can you use to hold the weight of the long hair in position?
14 How do you set ringlets?
15 Name two things that are different between combing out a short-haired hairstyle and combing out a long-haired hairstyle.
16 Name four precautions when cleaning and setting light-coloured postiche.

Colouring and perming postiche

This work is advanced wig dressing. It is practised only by experienced postiche dressers.

Hand-made real hair postiche

Colouring and perming can be carried out on postiche made of real human hair in much the same way as the hair on your head.

The precautions that you must take are:

1 You must not cause the foundation to shrink.
2 You must not cause the foundation to stretch.
3 The solutions used must not weaken or harm the foundation.
4 The extra wetting must not loosen the knotted hair.
5 It is always wise to carry out a strand of hair test.
6 The postiche must be firmly blocked up on a protected malleable block of the correct size for that postiche.
7 If there is drawn-through work, it must be protected.

Hand-made postiche is expensive, and because of this extreme caution should be used. However, a hand-made postiche usually has a long life. Clients find that old wigs lighten in the sun, and so are ready to have them coloured even if this means marking the foundation with dye. Perming and high and low lights are also popular.

Stock wigs that are stored by theatrical and film wigmakers for hiring out often have to experience change of colour and curl. Note that human hair never wears out, only the foundation that it is attached to.

Synthetic postiche

Colouring only can be carried out on synthetic fibre postiche. Cold nylon dyes can be used.

The same precautions must be used as for hand-made hair wigs, but are less stringent because these wigs are usually weft wigs made on an elastic base. They are also a great deal cheaper and easier to replace.

Some do have drawn-through work in the front, and this must be dealt with expertly so as not to colour the parting silk.

Work of this type is not in such demand for synthetic fibre wigs owing to their short life. However, they can be dyed into fun colours for fantasy work.

Trimming and shaping postiche

Hand-made real hair postiche

A wig that has been hand made for a client will have used hair as near as possible to the lengths of the chosen style. This is to avoid waste and loss of any natural curl. Trimming should be minimal, and is carried out with the wig on the client.

A hand-made real hair stock postiche might be made using only medium-length hair, and will then need styling to a client's requirements:

1 First check the fit, and cut in the base line for the hairstyle required on the client.
2 Remove the wig and block up on a malleable block. Wet down the hair enough to enable you to restyle the hair.
3 Set or blow dry into style.
4 Call in the client again and fit the finished postiche. If any alterations to the style are required, do them now.

This work requires experience in cutting and styling. Wigs will never grow, so if a mistake is made it will be an expensive one.

Film and media postiche often have fine knotted hair-lace hairlines, and because of their construction have to be blocked up carefully before they can be cut and styled. The fronts of these wigs are often changed, for example if a wig requires a short curly front and long hair at the back, or if the front of a short-haired wig must be worked in with a long-haired back. Cutting of hair is avoided most of the time because it is so expensive; it is cheaper to change fronts and backs than to cut off the hair.

The main exception is the cutting and styling of men's toupees. This cutting has to be done on the client's head in order to carefully graduate the postiche hair into his own hair. It is best to curl and blow dry the false and real hair together. This is made easier because you are working with short hair.

Synthetic fibre wigs

These have a short life owing to the elastic foundation, which perishes and causes the hairstyle to drop over the face and into the nape. Clients often require you to trim and reshape these wigs.

Precautions are:

1 Never use your *hair* cutting scissors.
2 Advise the client that you will be removing the curl and cannot make the hair curl again.
3 Advise the client that it would be better to adjust the foundation, in which case she will not lose the curl.
4 Advise the client that it may be time to order a new wig.

Hand washing

Wigs for hand washing are those made of synthetic fibre or machine weft.

Equipment

Two plastic bowls.
Two hand towels.
Shampoo.

Method

Follow maker's directions if you have them.

1 Fill bowl with warm water and a little shampoo.
2 Turn wig inside-out and place under water.
3 Squeeze the foundation several times. Do not rub.
4 Fill second bowl with clean cold water and rinse.

5 Repeat the rinsing. Do not rub.
6 Place the wig in a towel and squeeze carefully to remove excess moisture.
7 Take the wig out of the towel and shake.
8 Leave to dry either on a dry towel or on a head shape. Do *not* use heat to assist drying.
9 When dry, comb out carefully. Start at the nape (points to roots) and work up to the front hairline.

This type of wig requires no setting.

If the wig is machine-wefted Asian hair which has been treated to remove the cuticle layer, then you can set and style it. Dry in a postiche oven or under a hair dryer, or blow dry. These wigs often carry a label which states that they are made from 100 per cent human hair.

‖ Special effects

Blocking out hair

Eyebrows

The requirements are:

- to flatten the hairs against the skin so that they stay down for the duration of the performance
- to conceal their colour
- to change the shape and size, and to remove for clown or fantasy make-ups.

Method for stage use

1 Prepare non-irritating soap in advance. Cut it into little pieces, place the pieces in a medium-size jar, pour water over and screw the top on the jar. Leave the soap to go mushy (soft but still firm).
2 Clean brows first to be free from grease.
3 Rub or use brush on the brows and cover well with soft soap. Comb the brows flat, then slide a finger over them to smooth them down flat.
4 Dry the soap with a hair dryer. Protect the model's eyes and face.
5 Repeat this process as many times as required to reach a smooth surface which covers the brows with a smooth screen of dried soap.
6 When the soap is very dry, apply a film of sealer. Spread the sealer beyond the soaped area.
7 Cover with greasepaint or cream stick, blending carefully into skin edges to match foundation colour.
8 Press powder into the make-up, removing excess carefully with a damp patter.

You can now remodel your eyebrows for character or fashion make-up. Examples to try include:

- wide
- narrow
- male to female (dame make-up)

- add crêpe
- ballet dancer
- clown
- animal
- oriental.

Other methods

1 You can buy Derma wax for blocking out hair.
2 You can buy an eyebrow plastic stick which you use to stroke the eyebrows firmly and repeatedly in the direction in which they lie until they are flat. Sealer is then applied, followed by the foundation colour.

Figure 11.1 *Ageing a young man. Hair soaped out to give balding effect: loose hair stuck to edge of dried soap to cover remaining dark hair*

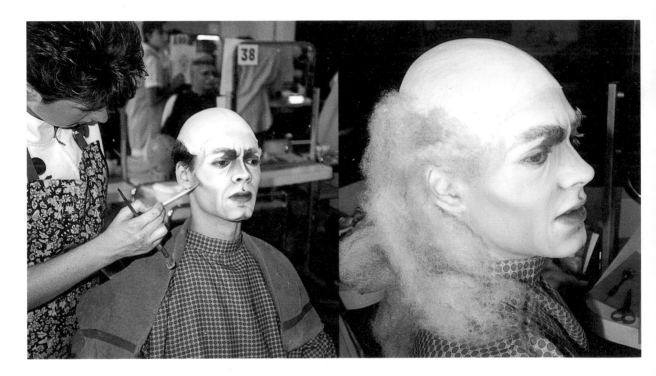

Other blocking-out projects

You can experiment with the blocking out of hair:

1 You can block out sideburns and temple hair to make a Joan of Arc character.
2 You can block out front hairline to give a very high forehead.
3 You can block out hair to make a bald pate effect by just taking out the front hairline back to the crown area (Figure 11.1).

With all these you must work one layer at a time and dry with a hair dryer before applying the next layer.

When the areas are all soaped down and dry, small areas merely need sealing. Larger areas need to have some very fine nylon stocking cut to shape and stuck down with spirit gum around the edges. The stocking is then covered with soap, dried, covered with greasepaint, and then powdered. Stipple sponge with coloured foundation.

Changing the shape of a nose

Design

Make a profile sketch of the shape of nose you require. If you have a profile photograph of the person you can trace that first. The nose must appear to be an integral part of the face. It must be blended into the natural skin so that no joins show.

Method using nose putty

1 Cleanse the skin free of grease and make-up. Rub witch hazel over the nose area.
2 Coat fingers with a little KY lubricating jelly. This will stop the nose putty sticking to your fingers. Take a small piece of putty and knead it until pliable. If it is very hard, place it on a radiator to warm it.
3 Stick the small softened ball of putty on the part of the nose that is to be built up the most (Figure 11.2). Press down hard for good adhesion. If it does not attach securely, remove it using some thread: pass the thread between skin and putty. This time paint the nose with spirit gum and let it dry. Now reapply the putty.
4 Always confine the putty to a small area. Keep it off the areas surrounding the nose. Always model the putty towards the centre of the nose; do not pull the putty outwards if you can help it. Carefully blend the edges of the putty into the skin. You can use a modelling tool or your fingers.
5 When the blending is finished, make final adjustments to the shape using mirrors to check the nose from both sides. Keep pressing and shaping with your fingers. Finally rub the putty with lubricating jelly, which will help eliminate unintentional cracks and bumps and give a smooth surface.
6 When you are satisfied with the shape of the nose from the front and sides and that the jelly has dried, decide now if

your character requires texturized skin. If it does, take a coarse black stipple sponge and press it over the putty. You can use the skin of an orange or lemon to good effect.

7 Now cover the putty and edges with some sealer. Remember to protect the eyes.

8 Stipple base colour over nose and face until it matches. If colour matching is not satisfactory, stipple several base colours over the nose lightly. Then powder very well. Set the powder.

9 A little powder rouge brushed over the end of the nose and nostrils sometimes helps.

10 If covering putty on the nose is difficult, try using some rubber-mask greasepaint to cover it.

Removing putty

Remove putty using a thread of cotton or silk held between two hands. Pull the thread over the skin under the putty. The putty comes off easily. The little that is left will rub off with some cleansing cream and a tissue.

Other uses of putty

1 Make a protruding chin.

2 Make a swelling, for example over and along an eyebrow. The putty allows you to make a cut in it to create the effect of an old scar, or of a fresh wound (to which some blood can be added).

3 Make warts with protruding stiff hair.

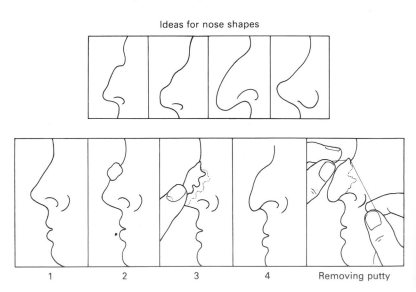

Ideas for nose shapes

1   2   3   4   Removing putty

Figure 11.2 *Using nose putty*

It is best not to place putty where you have a great deal of movement on the base.

Make-up for broken nose

The nose can also be altered with make-up. Figure 11.3 shows make-up for a crooked or broken nose.

Figure 11.3 *Make-up to give effect of crooked or broken nose: straighten by reversing procedure*

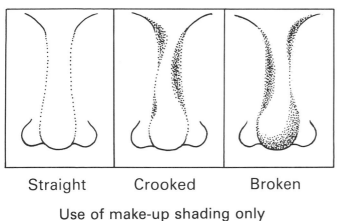

Straight   Crooked   Broken

Use of make-up shading only

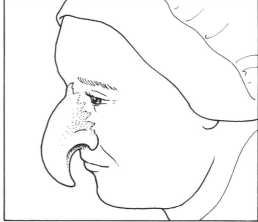

Latex nose – three dimensional

Assessments

1 Fill in work sheet for a Halloween witch.
2 Design a nose for the witch.
3 Design aged make-up for the witch.
4 Design aged hands for the witch.
5 Finish with a pointed witch's hat and wig.
6 Photograph before and after.

Burns, wounds, scars and welts

Powdered gelatine mixed with hot water provides an efficient means of creating such three-dimensional effects. The method is cheap and does not require great precision in modelling. Other scar methods are covered later in this chapter.

Take care. Boiling water is used, so mix the water and gelatine safely away from the model. The mixture makes a thick liquid which solidifies as it cools. You must work rapidly, as once it has congealed on the skin it cannot be reshaped. Be careful not to get the mixture into the eyes.

Equipment

Box of gelatine sachets.
Kettle of water.
Spoon or modelling tool.
Spirit gum.
Bottle of blood.
Tube of English mustard.
Scissors.
Powder.
Damp patters.
Make-up box.
Brushes.
Small bowl.
Spirit gum remover.
Protective gown.
Towel.
Eye dropper.

Method

1 Gown and protect the model.
2 Cleanse the area of skin to be covered in order to remove grease and make-up.
3 Dry the skin thoroughly.
4 Take one tablespoon of gelatine from the gelatine sachet and place into a small bowl.
5 Boil the kettle away from the model.
6 Now add hot water a little at a time to the gelatine powder. Stir quickly with a spoon or modelling tool, allowing it to cool a little until it is thick and syrupy. Check it is not too hot for the skin.
7 Then immediately apply to the skin area. Apply only as much as you think you will need. You can spread it a little before it cools.
8 When it is cool, powder it well then set with damp patter.

When it is cool you can cut it using scissors. Cut into the middle of the gelatine carefully, lifting it a little from the skin. You can now think up effects. For example, you can add make-up and place blood inside with an eye dropper for a wound, or use English mustard for pus and boil effects. You can insert nails, glass etc.

If the gelatine lifts off in places you can stick it down with spirit gum.

To remove gelatine

If you have placed it on the face, most models like to wash it off in warm water at a basin. If it is on the leg or arm, you could soften it with warm water from a bowl and then pull it off in large pieces.

Some ideas for you to try

1 You can colour the gelatine with food colouring, or mix in powder rouge.
2 If you would like a mottled effect, add seeds, oat flakes or lentils.
3 Gelatine can be used in a mould for more exact shapes such as eye pouches and scars. These are used cold and fixed with spirit gum. Caution: they can melt if used in a very hot atmosphere, e.g. under stage lights.
4 Moulds can be made by using plasticine or clay.

Skills that you learn with gelatine give you practice for working with latex. Latex achieves similar effects but is more durable (see later in this chapter).

Perspiration

Equipment

Small water spray.
Glycerine.
Gown for model.

Method

1 Place a little glycerine on the area you want to appear to be perspiring.
2 Now spray water on to the area over the glycerine.

Tattoos

1 Design and make a lino-cut of the type of tattoo required. Remember that it is back to front.
2 Stamp the lino-cut on to the skin area.

3 Clean off excess ink using cotton wool bud with acetone.
4 With fine brush, sketch in the colour if required.

Bruises and black eyes

Bruises take time to develop, so it is important that you know the time span you are covering when using make-up for a bruise.

Physical damage is noticeable after an accident only if:

1 The skin has been broken.
2 The blood makes the wound very apparent.
3 The muscles or bones have been damaged, in which case swelling will form.

In time the damaged blood vessels will discolour the skin surface and create a bruise.

A freshly bruised eye is red, with a little white at the centre of the bruise.

After 4 hours the bruising will travel to the inside of the eye socket, with secondary coloration underneath the eye and eyelid.

After 24 hours the bruise becomes darker, and purple has set into the eye socket area. Secondary coloration such as blue appears on the end of the bruise. Swelling will be apparent, so try to give a lump appearance by highlighting the centre.

After 48 hours the bruise becomes grey in the centre. It then gradually shifts to bluish red, to blue, to bluish green, to green, to greenish yellow, and to yellow.

Remember that the fresher the bruise, the redder it is; the older the bruise, the yellower it is. Watch your own bruises develop and make colour notes.

Black eye make-up

The numbers in the following refer to Figure 11.4. Use separate brushes for each colour.

1 Paint crimson in the deep corner of the eye socket.
2 Paint crimson under the eye pouch.
3 Paint blue/grey under and alongside 2. Paint blue in eyebrow and suggest circle to under eye pouch.
4 Fade out crimson into a reddish colour.
5 Use greenish tinge under eyebrow.

6 Use yellowish tinge merging out from the green close to the corner of the eye, above and below.

If the eye looks too colourful, take a fine stipple sponge and lightly stipple over the eye.
  Powder and set with damp patter if you want it to look like an old bruise. If you want it to look fresh, moist and inflamed, do not powder.

Scars

Effect 1

This method uses collodion of the non-flexible or new skin type. Alternatively you can use latex. Do not use around the eyes or on sensitive skin.

1 Gown model.
2 Clean and dry skin area to be used.
3 Paint collodion or latex on to area. The skin will contract slightly, leaving a scar.
4 You can just powder to make it look like an old scar.
5 You can use make-up to make it look like a new scar.
6 You can make a cut into it carefully to make a fresh cut.

To remove, use acetone or peel off carefully.

Effect 2

1 Spread area with spirit gum and dry.
2 Spread mortician's wax on the skin with a spatula.
3 Cover with sealer.
4 Cut into wax with side of spatula.
5 Brush inside cut with red greasepaint.
6 Add foundation and powder.
7 Add blood if required.

Make-up

Cuts and scars can be achieved using make-up only: see Figure 11.5.

Grazes

1 Use a tube of Tuplast, gelatine or latex. Spread the chosen substance on to the skin area.

2 Take a cocktail stick or orange stick and roughen the surface by rubbing it backwards and forwards over the substance.
3 Leave it to dry.
4 Take a brush and apply red make-up into the grooves.
5 Or take a small sponge with blood and pass over the rough area. This gives a fresher finish.

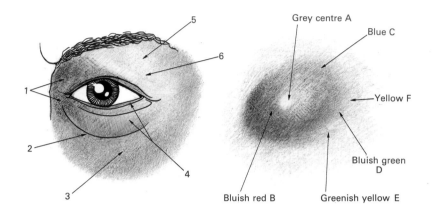

Figure 11.4 *Make-up to give black eye and bruise*

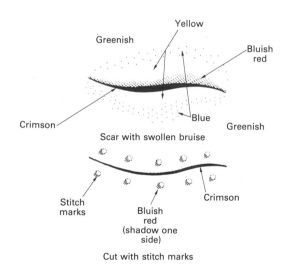

Figure 11.5 *Cuts and scars using make-up*

Temporary greying of the hair

There are two methods:

Talcum powder is used for amateur productions only. It gives a lifeless appearance but also shakes off the head easily.

There are temporary hair sprays in a range of colours. You must protect the face make-up when spraying. The sprays are quick and easy to use, and come out when the hair is washed.

Teeth

Under no circumstances should tooth enamel be applied to dentures or capped teeth.

First dry teeth with tissue. Apply enamel to the required teeth, using the brush fixed to the bottle.

Black is used to black out the teeth so it looks as though there are no teeth. Brown is used for discoloration; white for the healthy look; nicotine for the heavy smoker.

Assessments

1 Fill in work sheet for creating an accident victim.
2 Show the following effects on your model:
   - burn
   - bruising
   - cut
   - loose skin
   - lost teeth
   - lost blood.
3 Photograph before and after. Try to show each effect in your photographs.

Latex and applications

There are various brands of latex. Some are for use on the face and skin, and others are used for making bald caps and prosthetic pieces. Make sure that you use the right type.

Some brands of latex suit some people's skins while others do not. If you plan to use latex on a model, try it on the skin well in advance of the time required. If the latex feels as though it is burning the skin, *do not use it*. You should try another brand or a different technique.

You can buy clear or coloured latex for use on the skin. Clear latex can be coloured by the addition of concentrated dye, food colouring or even make-up powders. All these can be used to create the skin tone you require. Coloured latex is already coloured when you buy it, but it dries darker.

Ageing effects

Precautions

1 If your bottle of latex has a brush in the cap, always return the cap as quickly as possible. Once latex dries on a brush it is ruined.
2 Do not allow latex to get into the hair, eyes, eyebrows, eyelashes or beards.
3 If eyebrows are to be covered, block them out first.
4 If soft facial hair is to be covered, lightly oil or grease the skin then powder well.
5 If the skin is sensitive, coat it lightly with oil then use powder.
6 Protect the model well with a gown, and protect hair etc.

Equipment

Clear latex.
Coloured latex.
Plastic bowl.
Hair dryer.
Rubber-mask greasepaint.
Aquacolour make-up.
Spirit gum and spirit gum remover.
Red rubber sponge.
Gown.

Method 1

1 Apply ageing make-up. Powder and set make-up: it must be dry.
2 Apply clear latex with your fingers, working on one area of the face at a time. Pull the skin tight with your fingers and hold. Use a red rubber sponge and stipple the latex over that area.
3 Dry this area with a hair dryer.
4 When that area is dry, dust it with powder, then release the skin. The skin should form wrinkles.
5 If you want deeper wrinkles, apply additional coats of latex in the same way.

Method 2

1 Apply coloured latex, working on one area of the face at a time. Pull the skin tight with your fingers and hold. Use a red rubber sponge and stipple the latex over that area (you can use your fingers).

2 When that area is dry, dust it with powder and then release the skin.
3 Now you can do your ageing make-up, using rubber-mask greasepaint or aquacolour.

Removal of latex

The latex will peel off easily. If you have used spirit gum to stick down any edges, use spirit gum remover to soften it first.

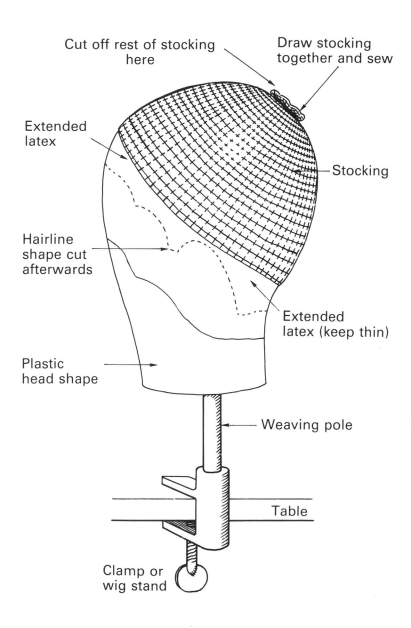

Figure 11.6 *Bald cap suitable for knotting hair on*

Plastic cap for balding

Equipment

Latex for making caps.
Black plastic or ceramic head of a suitable size. Check circumference of model's head. Check depth of head from front to nape.
Clamp and weaving pole or wig stand (Figure 11.6).
Powder.
Scissors.
Old brush.

Making the bald cap

Use a well-ventilated workroom.

1 Put the head shape on to a wig stand, or use clamp and weaving pole.
2 Paint latex on to the head shape.
3 Leave each layer to dry naturally.
4 Repeat this process three or four times, depending on the thickness required. Remember to keep the edges thin.
5 When well dry, powder the top side of the cap well.
6 Peel off the cap very carefully. Start at the nape and work forward. It is best to sit down and do this removing in your lap. Powder the inside and outside thoroughly as you roll it back; this prevents the cap sticking to itself.
7 Powder inside and outside again. This is now ready to use.

Putting on the bald cap

This method uses acetone, so ventilate the workroom well.

1 Wet the model's hair and comb it as flat as possible.
2 Ask the model to place both forefingers against the temples.
3 Pull the cap, starting from the front forehead, down over the head and the model's fingers.
4 Measure the size of the model's ears and make holes for them.
5 Remove the cap and cut it to shape.
6 Replace it on the head and pull it down well into the nape.
7 The model's fingers can be removed now.

8 Check the hairline and cut the cap to shape around the ears. Be careful to keep a good coverage of the hairline. Do not cut the cap too short.

9 Use spirit gum painted around the hairline, first on the forehead and then on the temples. Stick down the edges of the cap smoothly using a damp sponge.

10 Stick the nape down last.

11 The edges of the cap can be dissolved by acetone, which helps you to achieve a perfect invisible join. Be careful not to get acetone into the eyes.

12 You can now use make-up to finish the effect.

13 Powder well.

Making a bald cap for knotting hair

Refer to Figure 11.6.

1 Take the plastic head and place it on a wig stand.
2 Take the top of a nylon stocking and place it well over the head shape. Make sure the forehead and front have no pleats.
3 Sew the stocking tightly together at the crown, then cut off the remainder.
4 Paint over the latex using the same method as before. Extend the latex over the edge of the stocking.
5 Complete three layers.
6 Powder well.
7 Hair can now be knotted into the latex and stocking.
8 Hair can also be stuck or sewn on.

This cap can be used to make a receding hairline. It may be prepared as a clown's wig, using coloured crêpe hair or nylon fibre.

Removal of bald caps

1 Soften the edges of the cap with spirit gum remover on a flat small brush.
2 Now ease up the edges of the cap all around the hairline, carefully using the brush. Be careful not to let remover run into the model's eyes. Give the model a towel to hold up to the face to protect the eyes.
3 Lift the cap from the nape first and pull it forward to remove it. Any spirit gum left on the cap should be cleaned off with patters of cotton wool and spirit gum remover.
4 Powder the inside of the cap and place it on a plastic head shape.

5 The make-up will have to be cleaned off using alcohol or spirit gum remover.
6 If the cap is handled carefully it can be used again.

False nose using latex

Equipment

Box.
Petroleum jelly.
Plasticine clay.
Latex.
Modelling tool.
Powder.

Method

1 Model a nose with clay or plasticine. Check that the size will fit the model's nose. Place the nose into a small box facing upwards.
2 Grease plasticine nose with petroleum jelly.
3 Pour a little latex into a plastic bowl in a well-ventilated room.
4 Apply the latex with your fingers stroking the nose, and so covering all the nose shape once.
5 Leave to dry. Proceed in this way until three thin coats have been applied.
6 When dry, powder well. Proceed to peel off the latex nose from the plasticine. Remember to powder the inside as you peel off.
7 Remember to cut nostrils for breathing.

You can make other warts and bumps in the same way.

Application of false nose

1 Cleanse skin: there must be no grease on the face.
2 Try it on the model's face first to see how well it fits.
3 Trim any adjustments but keep the edges uneven and thin.
4 Paint inside nose edges with spirit gum.
5 Leave it to go tacky.
6 Place latex nose on to model's nose and press firmly.
7 Blend the edges into skin using acetone, making sure that there are no wrinkles by using a small towel if necessary.

8 Apply rubber-mask make-up: stipple on using more than one colour.
9 Powder and set (see Figure 11.3).

Removal of false nose

The method is similar to that for removing a bald cap.

Other uses of latex

Latex can also be used to create burns, scars and cuts. It can be painted over joins to make them invisible. See also Figure 3.14, page 38.

Assessments

1 Fill in work sheet for creating an ageing character.
2 Age male or female using latex.
3 Age hand using latex.
4 Make a bald cap.
5 Photograph before, during and after processes.

---

12 Making facial postiche

Moustache

Pattern and foundation

Draw the outline of the moustache area with an eyebrow pencil on to the top lip area. Take some tracing paper and place it over the area drawn. Trace the outline on to your tracing paper. This is your pattern.

Place this pattern on to a block and secure as follows.

If you only have a soft malleable block

1 Cut a piece of flexible card or plastic and place behind the tracing paper pattern before you fix it with pins to the soft block. This is only a precaution to stop the possibility of knotting hair into the canvas of the block.
2 Cut a piece of fine foundation net, making sure it is larger than the outlined pattern by 3 cm around the edges.
3 Place this over the pattern on the block and secure in place with a few pins.
4 Now take a long piece of plain tape and place pins next to each other all around the edge of the net so that it is held securely (Figure 12.1). This enables you to remove all the pins in one go without damaging the fine net or forcing the net out of shape.

If you have a hard wooden block

1 Take the pattern and either stick it on to the block or use sticky tape to hold it in place (always use a soluble glue that will wash off later).
2 Cut a piece of fine foundation net, making sure it is larger than the outlined pattern by 3 cm around the edges.
3 Place this over the pattern and use a staple gun to hold the net tightly over the pattern.
4 Alternatively use points. Points are very small straight nails which can be hammered into the block through the net. When they are halfway in, tap them sideways so that they lie flat on the block.
5 You will also need a pair of pliers for removing the points or staples.

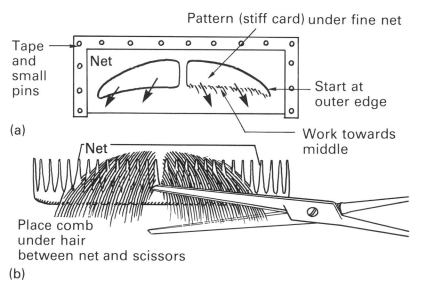

Figure 12.1 *(a) Blocking up a moustache pattern on a soft block; (b) trimming and styling a moustache*

Knotting

Start your single knotting from the bottom of the outer edges. Work towards the middle. Work both sides of a moustache simultaneously in order to give a balanced look (see Chapter 9 on knotting).

Work line by line depending on how thick you require the finish. You can turn the block upside-down to help with hair direction knotting. For example, every hole and every line produces a thick moustache; every other hole and every line produces a medium moustache; every other hole and every other line produces a thin moustache. Always stagger the knotting and use few hairs each time.

It is best to keep a natural effect. Thus, when you have nearly reached the top edges, it is possible to soften the line by using fewer knots or less hair, or even lighter-coloured hair.

If you want a natural lift to facial hair always knot in the opposite direction to the way it will be worn.

Trimming and styling

When you have filled in the moustache, remove it from the block by gently pulling the tape with pins in. Try it on your model before you trim and style.

Now place it on a soft malleable block and secure with tapes and pins. Take a dressing comb or a tail comb and place it under the hair of the moustache. Then trim with hairdressing scissors very carefully to the required length (Figure 12.1). You can use heated curling tongs to give added lift and movement. For a firm hold use setting gel.

You may trim the net edges at this time. Remember that the longer you leave the edges, the longer the moustache will last. The net wears badly on the edges. However, it must be invisible to an audience.

Beard

Before we srart with the pattern making of a beard, it may be appropriate for you to decide on a particular style of beard. It may be that your model does not have a distinct beard line for you to trace. Therefore, you must decide on the design of the beard line in advance. Your collection of pictures and photographs should help you with this.

Pattern and foundation

1 Draw the outline of the beard area with an eyebrow pencil on one side of the face only. Make a straight line from the centre of the middle lip going down to the beginning of the neck. Draw a line along the jaw outline from in front of the ear if sideburns are required as well (Figure 12.2, part 1).
2 Fold a piece of tracing paper in half. Place the fold on the centre line. Do not try to bend the paper under the chin yet. Place the paper so that it lies flat along the face back to the ear (part 2 of figure).
3 Trace the beard hairline on to the paper. Trace the jawline on to the paper. Remove paper after checking distance between jawline and neckline. Mark this.
4 Place tracing paper flat on the table and pin the folded piece to stop it moving. Now cut out the top beard hairline. This will give you both sides. Trim bottom edge to measurement. Cut vents at intervals up to the jawline; this will allow the pattern to mould to the face.
5 Place pattern back on to the face (part 3 of figure). Ask model to hold pattern at the ears.
6 Now mould the pattern under the chin carefully. Hold the shape with adhesive tape (part 4 of figure). Trim off any excess paper.
7 Find the right size chin block. If you cannot find a perfect fit, pad out the shape with papier mâché pads made by building up small pieces of wet paper until the shape is right. Allow the pads to dry hard before fixing the net.
8 Remove adhesive tape carefully. Lay paper pattern flat and cut out net shape flat, allowing extra for the edges. Place pattern on block first and secure with adhesive tape.

9 Attach the net using the same methods as for moustaches, depending on blocks etc. The main exception is the area under the chin. The very fine net must be evenly pleated, drawing the net in from both sides of the face under the chin. This enables the rest of the net to sit flat on the face planes (Figure 12.3). These pleats can be secured with points until the single knotting which will hold the pleats has been done. Some people do secure the pleats beforehand by sewing them.

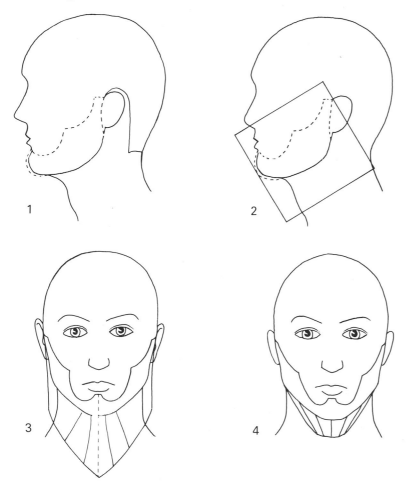

Figure 12.2 *Pattern making for a beard*

Hair

In the making of beards it is often more natural if you can divide the hair into three groups:

- dark hair: under the jaw and sideburns
- medium hair: above the jawline
- lighter hair for streaks etc.: finished hairline only.

Knotting

Turn your block upside-down and start knotting underneath the jawline (Figure 12.3). Work back towards the neck row by row. The hair must be knotted in a forward direction sticking out from under the chin.

When this area has been completed, start knotting straight down and travelling upwards and outwards on the chin and cheeks of the face.

The variations depend on the hair colour, style and thickness required. The variations can also depend on the amount of hair curl desired on the finished beard or moustache. Mixed Asian hair and crêpe gives a good finish. For a full beard, knot hair up towards nose, then comb back.

When the beard and sideburns have been completed, remove them and try them on the model's face.

Trimming and styling

Now trim and style the beard to the shape you chose at the beginning. Remember to leave good edges on your net foundation.

Ordering facial postiche

Figure 12.4 shows an order form for facial postiche. For the beard, measurements 1, 2 and 3 are indicated on Figure 12.5. Useful additional measurements A–E are also shown.

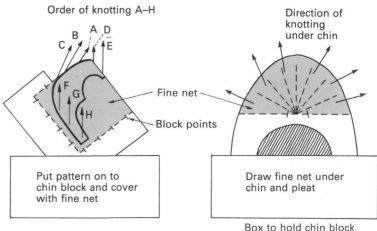

Figure 12.3 *Knotting a beard*

Name _____

Reference number _____

Address _____

_____

_____

_____

Production and period _____

Date order required _____

Date _____

Beard

Complete paper pattern then record following measurements:

1 From under bottom lip to just above Adam's apple. } See Figure
2 From centre of chin straight out to jaw pivot point. } 12.5
3 From jaw pivot point to top of ear line.
4 State length, texture and amount of curl required.
5 State style required: small, medium, large.
6 Indicate range of colour and attach colour sample.
7 Use tracing paper to make paper pattern.

B Moustache

1 Use tracing paper to make required pattern.
2 State length, texture.
3 State style.
4 Indicate range of colour or enclose a hair sample.

Beard shape/style   Moustache shape/style

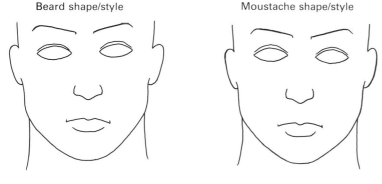

Figure 12.4 *Order form for facial postiche. See Figure 12.5 for measurement positions. 1–3 and A–E may also be required*

Application of moustache and beard

Moustache

1 Place in position, note the position and remove.
2 Take matt spirit gum and paint thinly on to the top lip area that was covered by the base net. Wait until it is tacky.
3 Place the moustache in position over the spirit gum and press into place using a small hand towel. Hold for a while, pressing down firmly. If any hairs are stuck down, lift them up with eyebrow comb.

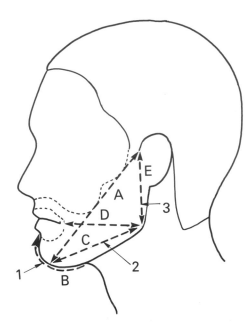

Figure 12.5 *Measurements for ordering a beard*

Beard

1 Place in position. Note position of hairline carefully and remove beard.
2 Paint matt spirit gum just below hairline and edge of beard under jaw. Allow it to become tacky.
3 Take the beard and carefully centre it on to the chin under mouth first. Then, working out from the centre, take each side and press down with a hand towel to secure. Use a fresh area of hand towel each time or you may spread the spirit gum on to the hair too much.
4 Secure at ear points.
5 Now secure under the chin and neckline, making sure that the beard is not wrinkled anywhere.
6 It may be that a little extra spirit gum will be needed on the hairline edge.
7 Hold and press down beard area with clean towel for a few minutes.
8 When dry, gently pull all hair in the beard. If it is secure, lift and comb it carefully into the style required. You must comb from the points to the roots carefully, in order not to tear the net. Start in the neck area and work upwards in layers if it is a very large beard.
9 Spray with lacquer if desired.

Dressing facial hair

You can wet it and set it if it is not what you require. You can curl it using heated, curling tongs or crimp it. You can trim and shape it with barber's scissors. Always protect the face with a comb held next to the skin/foundation.

Figure 12.6 shows a completed look.

Removal of facial postiche

1 Protect model's clothes with plastic gown.
2 Place towel under chin and around neck.
3 Pour spirit gum remover or alcohol (if not soluble spirit gum) into a plastic bowl.
4 Take a stiff brush like a large toothbrush and heavily soak the facial postiche net with the liquid remover. Be careful not to splash into the eyes. Do not rub or pull until the spirit gum has softened: rough treatment can irritate the skin as well as damage the net.
5 When the spirit gum has softened, the net will come away easily by itself.
6 Place it on one side until you have cleaned your model's face and made the model comfortable. If the skin is irritated, a very cold hand towel taken from a fridge and held to the face for a few minutes is very soothing.

Cleaning facial postiche

In a well ventilated room or outside in the open air:

1 Place postiche into a bowl of acetone to soak.
2 After some time, if the spirit gum and make-up still adhere to the postiche, gently rub the edge of the net only until it is clean.
3 Remove from acetone and leave to dry.
4 Pad out beard with paper to keep chin shape and store in a box along with your moustache. Or, in the case of repeat performances, the postiche can be placed back on to a chin block.

Knotted facial hair can be used many times if looked after properly.

Figure 12.6 *Example of knotted beard, moustache and sideburns*

Assessments

1 Carry out a full ageing make-up.
2 Complete the character by adding a knotted moustache and beard.
3 Take photographs before, during and after the application.
4 Add glasses or any other props.
5 Make several different types of moustache and beard to create different characters.

13 Character make-up examples

Figure 13.1 *Clown face*

Clown make-up

Equipment

Set up make-up trolley as in Chapter 1. Include:

Water-based make-up palette.
Grease-based make-up palette.
Clown white.
Talcum powder.
Large puff or powder brush.
Jar full of brushes.
Jar for used brushes.
Smooth stipple sponge.
Clown nose (ping-pong ball).
A latex cap.
Clown wig or hat.
Hair grips.
Hair Alice band.
Wet prepared soap in a jar or eyebrow plastic.
Hair dryer.
Camera for photographs before and after.
Sealer.

Method

Work to the sequence described for the clown in Figure 13.1. Remember that sequences change for different clown make-ups. You will understand the reasons for this when you have completed the make-up and experienced the problems.

1 Protect model with gown.
2 Cleanse face. Take photograph.
3 Comb and secure hair back from the face. Decide if you need a plastic cap for the head and forehead now. Protect the hair if not using a cap.
4 Block out the eyebrows with soap or eyebrow plastic. Dry well. Seal with sealer if the eyebrows are heavy.
5 Use a fine brush or eyebrow pencil to draw design accurately on to the face. Do *not* paint over these lines: it is

best to keep them so that the colours are separated and not touching.

6 Paint clown white evenly over the white part of the face. Use a sponge for large areas but use a brush near the lines. Do *not* paint white mouth now.

7 Powder the white make-up thoroughly with white talcum powder. Remove excess powder with damp patters and set the make-up.

In the following, remember to use one brush for each colour. This will keep your work clean, and the colours will remain bright and true. Do not touch the white base with any colour. For this water-based make-up, do not use very much water; this will give better coverage and control. Work quickly because it dries quickly. It will dry to a matt finish. It is not greasy, and so does not need to be powdered and set.

8 Take blue water-based make-up to paint in the eyes. If you have not used sealer over the soaped-out eyebrows then, because this is water-based make-up, you must be careful not to over-wet the soap. Just pat the colour with your finger tip in straight lines across the area: try not to go over the same area again.

9 Take the red water-based make-up and paint in the mouth.

10 The black-out lines are next. You must decide which make-up will make the best finish for you, i.e. greasepaint or water-based. Remember you will not be able to powder the black greasepaint. Paint these lines very carefully. The lines are free of make-up, so it should not be difficult. If you choose the right size brush for the width of the line, once over the outline should be enough.

11 Paint in the white lips with white lipstick.

12 Fix the clown nose into position.

13 Finish the total look by using a hat or a synthetic clown wig of a bright colour.

14 Take photograph of finished look.

Combination make-up works well for clown make-up. It gives you good line control and stops the face becoming over-greasy. It helps you to keep the make-up neat and comfortable for the model to wear.

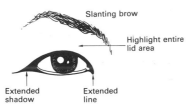

Slanting brow

Highlight entire lid area

Extended shadow

Extended line

Highlight under eyes to make them look puffy

TBA Fig. 13.2

Oriental make-up

Equipment

Set up work trolley as in Chapter 1. Include:

Soap in water.
Hair dryer.
Foundation of suitable colour.
Greasepaint palette.
Powder.
Powder puff or brush.
Lipstick palette.
Small piece of waxed paper.
Dermacil adhesive tape (clear plastic).
Scissors.
Liquid latex.
Stipple sponge.
Black wig.
Camera.
Sealer.

Method

1 Prepare model.
2 Cleanse face. Take photograph.
3 Soap out eyebrows or only part of eyebrows, whichever you think is best for your model. Dry. Apply sealer.
4 Apply base foundation such as yellow. Use a sponge to apply foundation.
5 To flatten the features, highlight these areas:
   - entire eyelid and eye socket right up to the eyebrow
   - under the eye and high cheek-bones
   - shadow under the bottom lip and chin area
   - outer edges of lips and also width of lips if rather full
   - nostrils of the nose and the shadows each side of the nose.
6 Apply shadow colour to:
   - make the jawline look round
   - flatten the nose by applying wide shadow right down the centre
   - make the forehead look rounded.
7 Apply powder generously. Remove excess with damp patters. '
8 Eyes: use black make-up (Figure 13.2).
9 Apply lipstick. Remember to keep the mouth neat and small.
10 If the character is old, you could use nicotine tooth colour to discolour the teeth.

Some models' eyes do not adapt easily to this make-up technique. For oriental eyes we can use three-dimensional effects as in the following section.

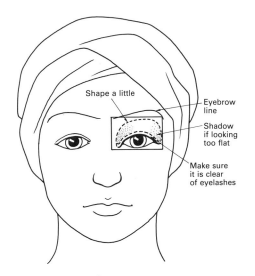

Shape a little

Eyebrow line

Shadow if looking too flat

Make sure it is clear of eyelashes

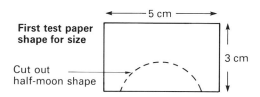

First test paper shape for size

5 cm

3 cm

Cut out half-moon shape

Figure 13.3 *Three-dimensional oriental eye effect*

Figure 13.4 *Example of stylized oriental make-up*

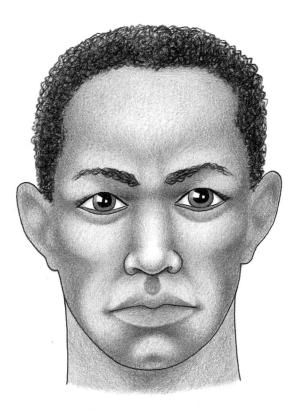

Figure 13.5 *Negro make-up*

Three-dimensional oriental eye effect

Refer to Figure 13.3.

1 Take a piece of thin waxed paper and measure off two identical rectangles 5 cm × 3 cm. Cut out.
2 Take a reel of clear plastic tape called Dermacil adhesive tape, 3 cm wide. You can buy this in a chemist's shop. Stick the tape neatly on to the two pieces of waxed paper.
3 Cut half-moon shapes out of the rectangles. If you can cut them out together they will be equal.
4 Try these in place over and behind the eyelashes. Trim to shape required.
5 Paint foundation on the eyelids; do not powder. This will stop the adhesive tape sticking to the lids.
6 Draw eyeliner along lid.
7 Peel off the tape from the waxed paper and stick into position over the eye socket. It should fit slightly slanting and under the eyebrows, if they have not been soaped out.
8 Complete both eyes. Make sure the model is comfortable with them.
9 Blend the edges lightly with a little stippled latex.
10 Dry with hair dryer.
11 Cover with greasepaint foundation. Blend in surrounding areas.
12 Powder well and wet make-up.
13 If the tape looks too flat, a little shadow can be added.

Finishing

Complete the oriental look with a wig of either modern or traditional hairstyle. Take photograph of finished look.

Geisha make-up

Figure 13.4 shows a completed stylized geisha make-up.

1 Draw a line around the face. Block out eyebrows.
2 Fill in face using clown white: make neat and even.
3 Powder and set base colour.
4 Draw oriental eye make-up as before.
5 Make eyebrows very black.
6 Draw small perfect lips in bright red.
7 Red blusher may be applied above eyes and on cheeks.
8 Make a head-dress or apply a wig.

Negro make-up

Equipment

Set up work trolley as in Chapter 1. Include:

Aquacolour water-based foundation.
A wig.

Method

Refer to Figure 13.5 (page 199).

1 Gown and prepare model.
2 Cleanse face. Take photograph.
3 Apply foundation with a sponge. Choose one of the aquacolour range, in order to learn another technique.
4 Highlights are applied a little differently this time. Take a clean damp sponge and, removing a little colour, lighten the following areas:
   - the forehead next to the hairline
   - the forehead above the eyebrows
   - eye curtain area
   - broadly on the top part of the cheek-bone
   - the wide length of the nose and edge of the nostrils
   - under the smile line, as in ageing make-up.
5 Paint around edge of lips with usual pale highlight colour. Fill in the top lip with deep coloured lipstick. Blot the lips with tissue. Highlight bottom lip and blot. Take some brown shaper and brush over the lips and the edges.
6 If you used a very dark foundation it will be difficult to make shadows. If not, take a darker foundation colour and shadow in the corners of the eyes and slightly down the side of the nose. Shadow and shape under cheek-bones. Take this down to the jawline at the side of the face. You can also shadow the neck.
7 Draw oriental eyes, but this time make a line all the way round the eyes.
8 Check model's ears, neck and hands.
9 Finish total look with a wig.

Take photograph of finished look.

Skull make-up

Draw a picture of a skull to work from (Figure 13.6). You can make it look stylistic or realistic. It makes you aware of the model's bone structure; feel the face carefully before you start.

Equipment

Set up make-up trolley as in Chapter 1. Include:

Aquacolour white or clown white.
Aquacolour shadow or clown shadow according to choice of white.
Make-up latex cap to fit model.
Spirit gum.
Talcum powder.
Powder puff.
Comb.
Wet soap in a jar.
Hair dryer.
Sealer.

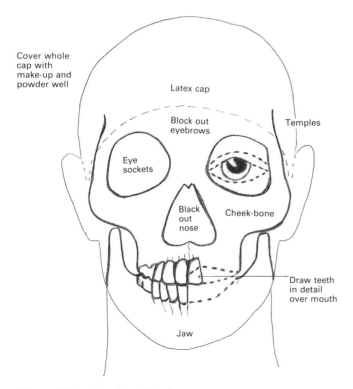

Figure 13.6   *Lines for skull make-up*

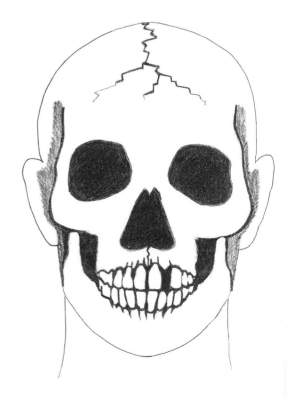

Figure 13.7   *Skull make-up*

Method

Refer to Figure 13.6.

1 Gown and prepare model.
2 Wet and comb model's hair flat. If long, let it lie down the neck. This can always be covered.
3 Cleanse face. Take photograph.
4 Apply latex cap (see Chapter 11).
5 Soap out eyebrows and dry (see Chapter 11).
6 Draw skull shapes on to the face. Use a thin brush or a soft eyebrow pencil. Draw teeth carefully.
7 Highlight the bones that protrude, and the teeth.
8 Shadow the hollows.
9 Highlight first, then powder well and set.

If you use water-based black then you will have a matt finish.
Try greens and blues for shadows. For horror effects, try blood or yellow gelatine.

This is quite a difficult make-up because you have to blend in moderation. Keep the make-up clear and well defined. Figure 13.7 shows a completed make-up sketch.

Place a black hood over the head to finish. Take a photograph of the finished look: try an additional black and white photograph.

Other character ideas

Figures 13.8–13.17 show some other ideas for character make-up.

Assessments

1 Design on work sheets in colour:
- tramp clown
- pierrot
- pantomime animal or Disney cartoon animal.

2 Work out the make-up sequence for each design. Areas to decide about are:
- colour of base foundations if any
- how many colours to use (no more than three)
- which type of make-up to choose: greasepaint, water-based, combination
- hat or wig to finish off the make-up
- the best sequence for applying the make-up
- whether a bald plastic cap is required.

3 Choose one design and complete on a model. Photograph before and after.

Caution: never use red make-up near the eyes.

Guidelines for all make-ups

Examiners will be looking for:

- artistic imagination
- detail ability in applying make-up
- blending of colours
- artistic use of colour
- finished result to be the same as your work sheet design
- good application and coverage of make-up.

You should maintain a high standard of hygiene as you work, for both yourself and the model. Remember that the examiner will be looking at you as well as your work and work area.

Figure 13.8 *Example of character make-up and use of crêpe hair, moustache and beard*

Figure 13.9 *Character make-up for a cat*

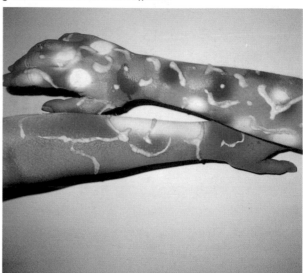

Figure 13.11 *An experiment with luminous body paint sprays: ground rice and water is also effective*

Figure 13.10 *Fantasy make-up helped by the use of a stencil and spray body paint*

Figure 13.12 *Changing a 17-year-old female student into a 30-year-old male Arab: and the same student with imaginative eye make-up*

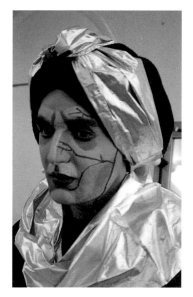

Figure 13.13 *Example of ageing make-up using a range of light and dark blue make-up. Very dark blue – shadows; medium blue – foundation; light blue – highlights*

Figure 13.14 *Alien character. A skull cap was used to cover the head first. Latex was moulded over a built-up rough surface*

Figure 13.15 *Example of horror make-up*

Figure 13.16 *Witch character make-up. An ageing make-up was completed after sticking on a latex false nose*

Figure 13.17 *Example of character make-up and use of crêpe hair, eyebrows and beard*

14 History of postiche and cosmetics

The requirements for the International Health and Beauty Council's examination and the City and Guilds wigmaking examination require you to have a general knowledge of the history of postiche and cosmetics from the seventeenth century to the present.

It is required that you research and prepare your own account of that history, covering hairdressing, postiche, other cultures' concepts of beauty, and the use of cosmetics. You are not required to write pages of information; brief notes will suffice. It is essential that you provide good diagrams and illustrations to show a varied selection of styles from each of the four periods. You need to state the reasons for particular styles and changes in styles, whether they be religious, political, social, change of monarch or fashion or other reasons. You also have to describe the construction of postiche, methods of dressing and materials used.

Seventeenth century

Cosmetics were widely used by men and women. Some examples of hairstyles are shown in Figure 14.1.

Women's cosmetics

Faces Whitened with powder, because dark complexions were considered common.

Cheeks The upper classes wore rose-coloured rouge, but lower classes wore ochre red.

Eyelids Covered with eye shadow, sometimes going up as far as the eyebrow. Colours preferred were blue, brown and grey.

Lips Coloured with rouge.

Patches These were pieces of black taffeta or paper, shaped like stars, half-moons and circles. They wore a great many of them at one time.

1640 English

Fontange

1690 French

Figure 14.1 *Hairstyles of the seventeenth century*

Women's hair

At the beginning of the 1600s wigs were worn. High foreheads were still considered beautiful, and women plucked the hair from their front hairline to achieve this effect. Some wore high head-dresses.

By 1615 they were wearing their own hair long at the sides, but dressed the rest into buns and coils on the crown. The fashion by men to wear lovelocks was copied by the women.

Full wigs for women were unusual, but in the middle of the century small added hair pieces were used over wire to make them stand out at the sides of the head only.

In 1696, a hairstyle called the fontange became popular in France. It was made of a high pile of false curls and many ribbons (Figure 14.1).

Men's make-up

Faces   They used flesh-coloured powder.

Lips   Fashionable men rouged their lips.

Patches   These were worn by fashionable men, whether they wore make-up or not.

Men's hair

It was the fashion to follow James I and wear one, two or even three lovelocks. These were very long sections of the hair that had ribbon tied at the bottom. Men wore then own hair long with a fringe at the beginning of the century.
When Charles II returned from exile, wigs for men took off rapidly. Men of distinction wore full-bottomed wigs, while tradesmen wore bobbed wigs. The men were pleased to shave their heads because the washing and hygiene of hair had been a nuisance.

Eighteenth century

Women's cosmetics

The use of make-up continued into this century for both men and women. It became very garish.
Women enamelled their faces with white lead paint. They were warned about the dangers of using this paint, which were that:

1 It caused the eyes to swell and become inflamed.
2 It changed the texture of the skin.
3 It attacked the enamel on the teeth.
4 In some cases the skin turned black.
5 Many women died because they used this type of make-up.

Women's hair

Women still wore their own hair but were showing interest in false curls which became very popular. Wigs were being worn by women who had lost their hair (hereditary female baldness was not uncommon in those days).

Women started to dress their hair over frames and shapes made of crêpe hair and then powdered the finished style. Curling irons were introduced to form rows of curls. Long hanging ringlets were popular and were made using switches, pin curls and marteaux (postiche hair pieces).

The middle of the century saw a bewildering change in women's hairstyles. Women had to resort to wigs, frames and all manner of false hair in order to create the most excessive hairstyles ever to be seen. Not satisfied with the height of the hairstyles, they embellished them with flowers, feathers, jewels and even a ship (Figure 14.2).

Hairstyles had to last as long as possible. Combing and brushing were impossible once the hairstyle was assembled. Washing the head was only executed about twice a year. Scratching sticks were a necessity as some of the heads were infested. Many women shaved their heads and wore complete wigs in the hairstyle of the day.

Hairdressing and wigmaking have never been as popular as they were then. The Académie de Coiffure, the first school of hairdressing and wigmaking, was opened in Paris by a M. le Gros.

By the 1780s sense prevailed and hairstyles became smaller and wider. The back was worn in a chignon and hung in a flat loop from the crown of the head to the shoulders. For a short time some women liked a mass of curls. Make-up also became more natural.

The French Revolution stopped the elaborate hairstyles and hair was cut and worn very short.

Men's hair

All the men continued to wear wigs as well as the ladies. Every town and village had a wigmaker. Men had a very wide range of styles to choose from; the three main categories were full and flowing wigs, bob wigs and short wigs with queues.

Beards and moustaches had lost popularity and were not seen.

1772

1700–1800

Figure 14.2 *Hairstyles of the eighteenth century*

Nineteenth century

The beginning of the century saw many changes for men and women.

Women's cosmetics

The fashion was turning to a natural look. Make-up had to be applied with art and taste. It had to be so subtle that it was often undetectable.

Cosmetics were sold under a new guise of creams and lotions to help the complexion. Ladies were advised to brighten a sallow skin. Face powder was acceptable. Later, eyebrows became darker, and mascara was introduced.

A German wigmaker called Charles Meyer developed Leichner's Theatrical Greasepaint Make-up at the end of the century. This started a slow revolution in make-up; actors and actresses used it both on and off stage.

Well bred English girls still did not wear make-up. Married women used to apply a little rouge to their cheeks, but no lipstick.

Women's hair

The taxing of powder in England brought about a dramatic change in hairstyles. In the Regency period, neat short hairstyles became popular.

The short hair soon lost its novelty and was discarded by the fashionable. Wigs were again in demand from women who could not wait to grow their hair.

Hairdressing and wigmaking had developed so much from the previous century that there were many well trained established hairdressers and wigdressers. The middle and end of the century saw an astonishing variety of hairstyles. Postiche wearing was so popular that a great amount of hair was required.

Women were wearing their hair in classical hairstyles again. The hair was dressed up into a chignon and plaited at the sides. Day styles were discreet but evening styles were very elaborate. Most women had long hair, but nearly all of them had a collection of hair pieces such as switches, pin curls, marteaux and diamond meshes. Many of these hair attachments would have been made from their own combings. This in turn matched their own hair colouring, so that women and men played guessing games as to whether the hair was false or true. Victorian society half pretended that false hair did not exist.

They used combs, plumes and ribbons to adorn these upswept hairstyles. Many elaborate chignons were kept dressed and ready for wear. The natural hair colour was all-important, and with that in mind hairdressers started to experiment with the use of colour.

In the last years of the century false hair was used less and less, except for women who were bald.

Men's hair

Wigs had stopped being worn except by servants and the legal profession.

Men wore their hair natural and unpowdered. It was fairly short in length. The younger men liked to comb the hair forward from the crown. Sideburns were popular.

In the middle of the century the front hair grew quite long and was allowed to touch the collar. A variety of side whiskers, beards and moustaches became the popular fashion. Barber shops became separated from hairdressers.

By the end of the century men's hair was cut short at the back but beards and moustaches came in all shapes and sizes.

Twentieth century

Women's cosmetics

At the beginning of the century, women still liked the natural look. They applied make-up more heavily, but used delicate colours. Natural nail polish was worn.

In 1920 the healthy tanned look became popular, with darker powders and orange lipstick. In fact, you could have a pale day lipstick and a darker night lipstick. In 1931 brighter coloured nail polish was available and women painted their toes. In the mid 1920s eye shadow, eyebrow pencil, mascara and bright lipstick became very popular. Eyebrows were being plucked into thin lines.

The 1960s brought extreme make-ups. White and pale lipsticks became the fashion. Eye make-up became very heavy, even Egyptian-like. False eyelashes were worn.

The 1970s were bizarre, and make-up became one big experiment: almost anything was acceptable. But reaction set in and everything went natural again. Tanny, muted colours became the fashion. In 1976 lips were outlined with make-up pencils and filled in using lip brushes, then covered with gloss. Eye shadow colours were silver, copper or gold.

Since then, it has mainly been the ranges of colour choice that have changed. Most women now wear make-up to look made-up.

Women's hair

The twentieth century was another bumper one for hairdressers and wigmakers. The range of hairstyles was tremendous.

The century started with the craze for auburn hair and the 'Gibson girl' pompadour hairstyle. They used crêpe hair pads to help with the fullness. These styles continued until the short bob in 1920. Women decided to go to barbers to have their hair cut off, instead of hairdressers. Wigmakers still kept up with the new short styles but charged twice as much.

Hair colouring was beginning to be acceptable. Hollywood was setting the style. Bleached platinum hair was news.

A long bob (page boy) was introduced and hair began to grow long again. Small false hair pieces were popular for changing from short to longer in the evenings. Marcel waving irons were used for waves and curls.

In 1945 hair was dressed off the neck again, into a bun, doughnut or French pleat hairstyle. In 1949 the cold perm arrived. In 1950 hair was worn long or short. Women went colour mad, using blonde, silver, red and bluish tints. Wigs of real hair and, for the first time, synthetic fibre were worn as fashion postiche.

In 1955 the bouffant hairstyle arrived, plus decoration. Rollers were introduced to set these hairstyles. Back combing became a necessity to gain the fullness required. By 1961, wigmaking establishments had become major industries. Practically every women in the country had at least one hair piece. They were accepted by everyone as fashion accessories.

By 1970 hair was long and smooth with the ends just curled up. Short styles were very curly all over (bubble cut). In 1971 Vidal Sassoon and his geometric cuts of short smooth free-flowing hair became popular with the young and beautiful. Fun and crazy wigs could be bought for parties.

In 1979 short hair was worn at the back and sides but the front hair was left longer and curled. By 1986 longer and fuller hair was fashionable. The hair was crimped with crimping irons or spiral wound on spiral curlers to give the Afro perm look. Hair gels and sprays were used to hold the hair in firm sets, or spiked or braided hairstyles. Dreadlocks and hair extensions became popular for making the hair appear fuller and longer. Long, full, natural fashion wigs came in again.

Men's hair

In 1895 the safety razor was introduced. Moustaches were unfashionable for young men. Men had their hair waved in the front, but the rest of the hair was short.

In the 1950s the crew cut (flat top) arrived. Next came the Elvis Presley hairstyle with sideburns. In 1958 there was a big demand for men's postiche and hair colouring. The 1959 teddy boy hairstyles were followed by the Caesar cut, better known as the Beatles hairstyle. Side partings were popular.

In 1964 men's postiche changed with the introduction of implanted hair into a soft flexible plastic base or a hard fibreglass base. You could swim in and wash these hair pieces, but they were not good for the scalp. The suction that kept them on was very strong. Some beards and moustaches became popular again. Hair was generally short and being worn in a variety of ways.

In 1977 some men wore long hair free or tied back at the nape (hippy style).

By 1980 hair was generally being worn short. There appeared some exotic extreme hairstyles like the Mohican, and the sides of the head were shaved back to the scalp on skinheads. Hair extensions called dreadlocks became popular. Hair gels and sprays were used to spike the hair to make it stand out or to give it a sculptured look.

Designs cut or shaved onto the hair showing the scalp reached us in the 1990s.

Modern wigs

Wigs today are worn for fashion, necessity and as part of official uniform in Britain. They are also worn for the stage, screen and television. Some are made of real hair but many are now made of synthetic fibre. Trichologists predict that the incidence of baldness will increase gradually over the years for women as well as men.

We will conclude that wigmaking and cosmetics will probably continue for a few thousand years more!

Assessment: historical research

Choose a project to build on your existing factual knowledge gained at basic level, and to show wider evidence of research into the sociological and technological reasons for changes in style and design. The project must show evidence of ability to re-create and document elements of these changes from some chosen period, movement or artefact. You are not required to write pages of information, brief notes will suffice. It is essential that you provide good diagrams and illustrations.

One topic might be the history of make-up and the different cultural concept of beauty. You may choose to discuss the features that different cultures consider beautiful. You may choose one culture to expand on. You may take one period in great detail, or give a brief history of the development of make-up through the ages up to the present day.

Reading and research are an important start to your work. Fashion and history have always walked hand-in-hand, for the one is a mirror of the other. To know your subject thoroughly you must understand its beginnings in order to keep up with the present. This is an ever-changing picture, but one that often repeats its past in a constant search for the 'new idea'. Watch film, television and theatre and note how the make-up, hairstyles and costume are applied. Learn from all you see.

The assessment criteria for projects will include: creative ability, originality, an imaginative approach, evaluation of media and resources, project analysis, development of ideas, and problem solving. Students' working methods should include research, organization of work, understanding and use of resources, the use and selection of tools, equipment and materials, and the application and attitude to tasks (see Figure 14.3).

Name ....

Title of project ....

Submission date ....

Please circle grade awarded at each stage of project

Date	Stage	Ability	Grades			
	Planning	Analysis	A	B	C	D
		Imagination	A	B	C	D
		Originality	A	B	C	D
		Comments				
	Organizing	Resourcefulness	A	B	C	D
		Selection of materials	A	B	C	D
		Anticipation of needs	A	B	C	D
		Comments				
	Performing	Skill	A	B	C	D
		Accuracy	A	B	C	D
		Efficiency	A	B	C	D
		Comments				
	Interpreting	Comprehension	A	B	C	D
		Judgement	A	B	C	D
		Open-mindedness	A	B	C	D
		Comments				
	Presenting	Style	A	B	C	D
		Literacy	A	B	C	D
		Numeracy	A	B	C	D
		Comments				

Figure 14.3 *Typical project assessment form*

15 Careers and business practice

Career planning

The following is a brief guide to jobs and careers within this industry.

Major theatre companies

Heads of wig and make-up departments require wigmakers who are trained in hairdressing and theatrical make-up. In general they like you to have A level English or to be well read and knowledgeable about the theatre in order to make character analysis. You may be expected to tour with the company.

Television companies

To apply for a position as a trainee make-up artist you would normally be required to have experience in hairdressing, wigmaking, wigdressing and beauty. They are also interested in A level art, English or history.

Make-up artists in television only maintain wigs by cleaning and dressing them. The making of wigs is carried out in a wig department, which supplies make-up designers with their requirements. It has been indicated that this structure may change in the future.

Regional studios, when they are in production, use wigs from stock, or purchase or hire wigs from theatrical and film wigmaking companies.

Freelance make-up artists

Many productions these days are by small film companies. They employ their own freelance specialists. Because they work on a smaller financial scale, they like to employ make-up artists with multiple skills, e.g. wigdressing, hairdressing, the making of facial postiche.

The productions are sold to the television companies. This

may prove to be a developing market as large television companies attempt to cut escalating costs by buying in most of their material.

The making of video films also comes under this heading; the requirements are similar.

West End theatres often require freelance make-up artists as well as wigdressers. A newspaper called *The Stage and Television Today* advertises these positions.

Commercial wigmakers

These produce wigs and toupees for private clients, and wigs for National Health Service clients. These postiche are for daily wear. The work consists of wigdressing, foundation making and knotting, and ongoing repair work.

Theatrical and film wigmakers

These make special wigs for specific productions. Both require wigmakers and wigdressers, full time and part time.

Hairdressing salons

Salons require staff who can take accurate measurements, and fit and dress a postiche. Orders can be taken for made-to-measure wigs or ready-made wigs.

Some salons have their own workrooms for wig and toupee making. Some hairdressers specialize in National Health work.

Department stores

Stores employ staff to demonstrate and sell ready-made wigs.

Remedial work

Private clients require help with camouflage make-up and/or the making and application of small postiche work. Cleaning and dressing of postiche.

Transplant industry

This area of work requires staff for knotting hair into the scalp and some hairdressing.

Marketing

Firms require salespeople for theatrical and cosmetic make-up sales and demonstration work.

Teaching

Lecturers are required in colleges for courses in wigmaking and in theatrical and media make-up and postiche work. Teacher training may be required.

Photographic make-up artists and hair stylists

This involves mostly fashion photography, including make-up, advertising and hairstyles. Top hairdressers are often the agents for make-up artists covering photographic work, and demonstrators for make-up products.

Madame Tussaud's

Madame Tussaud's is famous for creating lifelike wax figures. The exhibition was founded over 200 years ago in Paris.

The work of Madame Tussaud's studios is unique, and about twelve people are employed to work on hair, wax colouring and wigmaking. Super realism is attained by attention to detail and an understanding of colour, textures and form in relation to wax as a medium.

Madame Tussaud's requires you to be fully trained in hairdressing and the application of make-up, as well as possessing an artist's eye for colour and detail. Sometimes wigmaking and postiche skills are required. The specialised skills of implanting hair, the colouring of wax heads, and the creation of eyes are taught by Madame Tussaud's.

In addition to the above, the daily routine at Madame Tussaud's includes the maintenance of the waxwork figures. Regular cleaning of the faces and cleaning and redressing of the hairstyles keep the figures fresh and lifelike. The hairstyles range from modern to ornate historical styles.

Window dummy model wigs

These are shaped wigs, sometimes machine made.

Porcelain dolls' wigs

These are miniature wigs with hand-knotted hair which are glued to the porcelain heads.

Drama societies

People are needed to work within any drama production, whether it be professional or amateur.

Competition work

Hairdressing competitions, both national and amateur, require knowledge of make-up and postiche work, mainly in the 'fantasy' and 'total look' sections.

Film world

You must join a union to be employed in the film industry. You must have had previous experience in video and television work.

Prosthetics

The requirement for three-dimensional prosthetics is growing. The skills include:

- casting of face and hands
- modelling ageing head and hands
- making and applying foam latex
- making and applying false teeth, ears and noses.

This is advanced work requiring some knowledge of sculpture and an understanding of chemical formulae. Prosthetics can be specialized work on its own but will become more extensively used in theatre and television. It has already been widely used in the film industry.

Employment and work practices

Finding employment

What can you offer the public?

Make a list of all the things you have learned to make or do that you could sell.

Where can you sell this knowledge, and to whom?

Make a list of all the job positions you can think of.

How do they know you exist?

They do not know you exist?

What can you do about it?

Write letters.
Ring up employers.
Walk in and ask to see employers.
Try to get to know someone who already works somewhere.

If they want to see you

Before you go for an interview, find out as much about the workplace as you can. Identify what the employers sell. If you can make a suggestion to improve their sales, they will be impressed. They may require a curriculum vitae, so have one ready.

Take a photograph album of your best work. Take and show them the hair pieces that you have made. Explain carefully all the things you can do; do not assume that they know. They may ask you to block up and set a wig, or to make up a model.

Your own appearance should honestly reflect the type of person you are. Think carefully about how you present yourself. You are in the fashion business, and are judged in the first place by appearance and personality. Be happy; remember that clients do not want long faces, and in the theatre 'the show must go on.'

Hairdressers, wigmakers, beauticians and make-up artists are often content to rely upon skills alone to advertise their work. With increasing competition it becomes necessary to 'sell' service as well as goods. The more skills operators have, the more jobs are on offer to them. Employers may prefer an operator with multiple skills because they need only pay one person each week. This should be reflected by higher wages for the operator. The salon in turn uses the employee's multiple skills to offer a wider range of services and goods to the public. The need to let the public know about these skills necessitates advertising.

Keeping work and client records

You should record all the work that you complete:

1 Make copies of all your work sheets for make-up work.
2 Record all postiche orders: measurements, patterns and order forms.
3 Record your personal data.
4 Record all correspondence.
5 Keep a check on stock.
6 Keep an expenses record (bookkeeping).
7 Use photographic recording whenever possible.

These records are confidential to you. They must be kept in a safe place because you never can be sure when you may need them.

You can divide a filing cabinet up into different drawers for various sections of the above list. The cabinet should be locked when not in immediate use. Keep the contents in alphabetical order. Clients' personal information should be placed into strong large envelopes with their names, addresses and telephone numbers on the front. You could also have a serial number on each envelope. This could be used instead of a name when dealing with staff to keep the identity of the client confidential. If the work is for the theatre, film or television, confidentiality is not so important.

A computer can be used like a filing cabinet for recording most information. However, you would still need to store old patterns for postiche, hair colour samples and photographs, etc.

Ideas to stimulate sales

Modern advertising

Various manufacturers will advertise for you if you mainly sell their products.

You can advertise in the newspapers, by using circulars or posters, and on local cinema, television and radio.

It has been found that spasmodic advertising does not pay as well as continuous advertising.

Good window dressing

The public are attracted to a window that is changed regularly. They like artistic displays of show and light.

Naming

Place your business name on proprietary articles sold in the shop.

Buy in stock in small quantities

Wholesalers are always willing to help.

Best advertisement is recommendation

The public generally recognize a reliable worker or owner who generates confidence and believes in fair dealing with technical efficiency.

Have an open evening

Offer the public a free glass of wine. Put on a small fashion show with demonstrations of make-up and a variety of different coloured wigs for them to try on. This encourages new clients and enhances goodwill among the regulars.

Give talks and demonstrations

Offer talks to local societies, colleges and schools.

Have a large showcase in the salon

This can sell other products such as jewellery, stockings and hair ornaments.

Offer refreshments

Serve refreshments including tea and coffee.

The workplace

Offer a bright, clean and happy atmosphere. Nothing loses customers quicker than a bad attitude. Problems should be resolved when the public have left, or in private.

Staff

Staff should be encouraged to sell all products. They should be fully conversant with all the stock. They should know and understand about postiche and be encouraged to use postiche and hair extensions themselves.

Staff should realize that they have a responsibility to sell, even if the salon does not belong to them. It helps to safeguard the success of the business and the permanence of their jobs. Staff are usually offered a percentage of the selling price as an incentive.

Legal requirements

In order to work you must be aware of the law as an employer or an employee. The following Acts were passed by the government to make a safer working environment for people to work in. This section summarizes the requirements.

1961 Factories Act

This covers a variety of workplaces, not just factories. It requires that

1 Floors, passageways and stairs must not be obstructed.
2 Floors must not be slippery.
3 Equipment such as ropes and lifts must be carefully maintained.
4 Fences must be maintained.
5 There should be toilet and washing facilities.
6 There must be adequate lighting, suitable ventilation and a reasonable temperature.

1963 Offices, Shops and Railway Premises Act

Basic health and safety regulations are specified concerning:

1 Number of toilets required per number of persons.
2 Washing facilities.
3 Suitable rest areas in which to eat/drink/smoke.
4 Adequate lighting.
5 Floor space.
6 Working temperatures.
7 Space per person.

1969 Employers Liability Act (Compulsory Insurance)

This requires the employer to take out correct insurance. The insurance should cover accidents to themselves, their staff and their clients.

1974 Health and Safety at Work Act

This updates the 1963 Act.

1 It identifies the general health and safety responsibilities of the employer and the employee.
2 It requires first aid boxes to be available so that first aid can be given to a client or an employee.
3 It gives guidelines as to what should be included in the first aid kit.
4 Regulations relating to the reporting of accidents are also included. All accidents and injuries must be written down and reported.
5 Where fewer than 50 employees are at work, the employer has to provide an appointed first aider who also should frequently check the contents of the first aid kit.

1974 Fire Precautions Act

Fire precautions must be taken, including the provision of firefighting appliances in the workplace and adequate staff training in their use.

The premises must be approved by the fire authority for safe exit routes in case of fire (fire drills).

It is recommended to visit your local fire brigade's fire prevention department. They can advise you on careful use of materials, suitable types of fire-extinguishing equipment, staff fire training and the proper layout of premises for safety in the event of fire. All such advice is given free.

1977 Safety Representatives and Safety Committees Regulations

1980 Notification of Accidents and General Occurrences Regulations

1982 Health and Safety Regulations Update

A self-employed person has to ensure that he/she makes provision for rendering first aid to him/herself, or a client, while he/she is at work.

An employer must ensure that equipment and facilities are provided which are adequate for enabling first aid to be given to employees if they are injured or become ill at work. Employees have a duty to take care of themselves and others who may be affected by their acts. The criteria for deciding what provision is adequate and appropriate include the number of employees, the size of the establishment, its location, and the nature of the work.

Knowing the law

The law is enforced by health and safety inspectors. They can stop the premises being used if they are unsuitable. They can order improvements to the workplace. They can stop the use of equipment they consider dangerous.

It is therefore very important for you, the employer or employee, to know and understand the law and understand the part that you should play in it. When it comes to health and safety we are all responsible for each other.

Remember that if you decide to open a business you should consult a legal expert, as the notes I have given are intended for general use only.

Glossary

Postiche work

Adhesive patch   An area on the underside of men's postiche which is covered with oiled silk.

Angora hair   Hair from a goat; long and silky. Used in fantasy work

Beeswax   Used for sewing to stop the cotton knotting up. Used for weaving on the weaving silk.

Bigoudi   Wooden curler used for permanently curling the hair.

Bind ribbon   A wide piece of silk galloon which encircles the head on the underside of a wig mount.

Boardworker   Person who makes postiche.

Block   Wooden, suitable for mounting foundations of post-iche. Head shaped. Comes in various sizes.

Bracing   The cottons which hold the foundation in position on the wooden block during the knotting process.

Caul net   An open-weave soft net used on the crown area of a wig.

Chignon   A small woven or knotted hair piece. Worn as a bun, or figure of eight shape, between the crown and nape of the head.

Clamp   A tool that clamps to the table. It has a hole that will hold weaving poles upright.

Crêpe hair Hair that has been permanently crimped by weaving, boiling and baking.

Croquignole   Winding from point to root.

Diamond mesh   A method of sewing up weft into diamond-shaped meshes. The weft must incorporate one wire strand.

Double knotting   Knotting hair to a foundation net by forming two knots together for added strength.

Double-sided adhesive   A plaster which is adhesive on both sides. Used for men's postiche and beards.

Foundation   The base of any piece of postiche. Made of net, to which hair is attached.

Frisure forcée   A method of permanently curling hair, used in the making of postiche.

Hackle   A giant comb used to disentangle hair and for mixing hair for colour matching.

Hackling   A method of disentangling tangled hair.

Hair-lace   A very fine flesh-coloured mesh used to blend off hairlines where they meet the skin to give a natural hairline effect. The fine lace is covered with make-up. Mainly used for screen and the theatre.

Mount   The part of postiche that is made of net and galloon all sewn together.

Oiled silk   Used to protect the net foundation on men's postiche where adhesive is placed. Sometimes used to protect positional spring from rusting.

Points (wig points)   Headless nails used for forming and holding foundation to wooden block to ensure a good fit.

Postiche   A trade name given to any form of hair work from an eye-lash to a full wig.

Postiche clip   A clip for attaching pieces of hair work to the hair.

Postiche oven   A large oven which has a gentle heat similar to a drying cabinet. Used to dry postiche slowly overnight.

Springs   Can be prepared watch spring or specially manufactured springs. In either case they are used to hold the wig foundation in shape and position on the head.

Strings   The weaving silks on a weaving frame.

Teasing   The manual loosening of entangled hair before hackling.

T-pin   A large ordinary straight pin, but with a bar across the top so that it resembles the letter T. Without the bar it is called a postiche pin, used for setting postiche.

Turning   The process of arranging raw mixed hair until all the root ends are together, so that the hair will not tangle.

Ventilate   To postiche makers, this means knotting.

Ventilating needle   A knotting hook used for attaching hair to a foundation. Various sizes: the lower the number, the finer the hook and the fewer hairs taken at a time.

Trichlorethylene   A solvent used to clean postiche. The danger from this substance is that the vapour given off acts as an anaesthetic and is poisonous, so that a person who is overcome by the fumes may collapse, and faces the risk of death unless they are moved from the floor to a higher position. Cleaning must take place in a well ventilated position.

Yak   A kind of ox with long coarse curly hair.

Make-up

Acetone (nail polish remover)   A clear liquid solvent used for cleaning hair-lace and removing spirit gum. Has strong fumes: keep away from the eyes and keep tightly sealed, as it evaporates.

Alcohol   Rubbing alcohol can be used to remove spirit gum.

Beard block   A shaped wooden block used for knotting facial postiche. A plaster cast of a head can be substituted or made.

Body make-up   Available as a transparent liquid or a powder. It is applied with a sponge and removed with soap and water.

Crêpe hair   Used for making quick beards and moustaches and occasionally eyebrows etc. There are two types: crêpe wool and human hair crêpe. The crêpe wool is cheaper.

Eyebrow plastic   A stick of wax used for blocking out eyebrows.

Gelatine   Can be used for quick three-dimensional work. Available in boxed envelopes of powdered gelatine.

Hair dryer   Used to speed the drying time of soap and latex and hair.

KY lubricating jelly   Used for blending nose putty and Derma wax.

Latex   Used for creating wrinkled skin in the ageing process; for attaching crêpe hair effects; and for making small prosthetic pieces.

Latex caps   You can buy them already made, or make them yourself with Glatzan liquid plastic. You must not use this on the skin.

Modelling clay   Used to model features for prosthesis. Obtainable from art supply shops.

Nose putty   Used for building up noses and other shapes, like a hole for a bullet wound.

Plaster bandage   Rolls of bandage impregnated with plaster for use in making moulds with alginate. Can be obtained from art supply shops as well as chemists.

Plaster of Paris   Used to make positive casts and negative moulds.

Plastic head blocks   Used to make plastic caps.

Rubber-mask greasepaint   A special castor-oil-based greasepaint to use on latex.

Sealer or fixative   Used to provide a protective coating for various make-up constructions, e.g. putty noses, soaped-out eyebrows.

Soap   Mild toilet soap used with water to block out hair.

Spirit gum   A liquid adhesive. Buy the matt finish gum. Used for hair-lace postiche, latex caps etc.

Thread   Common sewing thread to remove putty from the face or skin.

Tooth enamel   Available in six colours.

Tweezers   Handy for attaching small latex pieces or facial postiche.

Wig block   Called malleable. Used for dressing postiche on.

Wig stand or holder   Used for holding malleable block while setting and dressing postiche.

Index